The Story of My Mother

Of Whom We Come And Whence We Came

P.P. Atte

To mother, thank you for letting me tell your story. I hope it honours you, your essence, and your spirit. I am eternally grateful that I come from you.

Inspired by my late dearest friend Kari Olesen 1972-2022

And always, Jordan & Chelsea, thank you for helping me evolve daily and see the world in new ways through your eyes.

"A mother is incomparable."
AFRICAN PROVERB

Contents

Main Characters

LYDIA ATTE (née BRISIBE) (1938- present). My mother.

OKPE BRISIBE (Unknown-2001). My mother's mother and her closest childhood friend.

FRANCIS BRISIBE ADAMAGU (Circa 1894-1972). My mother's father. He was a member of the informal House of Chiefs representing the Izon tribe under British colonial rule.

EBITOUBO (Birth and Death dates unknown). My mother's maternal grandmother.

WILLIAM AYAKEME ATTE (Circa 1932-2010). My mother's husband and my father. She married him on April 24, 1956.

SUSANNAH AREPREKUMOR (née BRISIBE) (1950-2019). My mother's sister.

ELAKEMFA (Birth and Death dates unknown). My mother's older maternal cousin who was like an uncle to her. He resided in Bomadi, and she spent many holidays with him and his household as a teenager.

SASI (Unknown -1986). One of my mother's former stepmothers and later became her sister-in-law.

ENAITORU (Unknown -1950). My mother's mother-in-law, whom she had never met.

MY MOTHER'S CHILDREN (My mother bore five children in 1961, 1965, 1968, 1970, and 1972 respectively, but is a mother to eight children, with seven still living).

AWIKI BRISIBE (1938-1978). My mother's half-brother and close confidant.

EFFIONG AKPAN (Whereabouts and status unknown). My mother's former '2iC' (Second-in-Command) from 1973 to 1979. She employed Effiong Akpan in 1973 in Port Harcourt as her household help, and he also became her 2iC in all her small business ventures, helping her. After six years, he left her household in 1979.

JANET ADEAGBO (Living) My mother's best friend from 1979-1982.

AJIMMY (Unknown -2019) My mother's nephew-in-law.

Places

OJOBO – My mother's hometown, located in Burutu Local Government Area, in Delta State, Nigeria. Coordinates: 5.0149° N, 5.6602° E.

PERETORUGBENE (popularly known as **Peretoru**) – My granny Okpe's hometown, also my paternal grandmother's hometown, and where my father grew up. Peretoru is now located in Ekeremor Local Government Area, Bayelsa State, Nigeria. Coordinates 4.9747° N, 5.6403° E.

BOLOUTORU CREEK is a channel in the Niger Delta, in southern Nigeria. It flows for approximately 198 kilometers (123 miles) and meets the sea at the Bight of Benin in Delta State, Nigeria, and it is known to the Izons as Boloutoru. People have been fishing on this river for years and then came to a dock on the Niger River to sell/store and use for personal consumption. Coordinates: 5°18'30"N, 6°25'0"E.

BOMADI – My maternal great-grandmother Ebitoubo's hometown. Bomadi is an Izon local government area in today's Delta State, Nigeria, with eleven communities. It is a town that lies on the bank of the Forcados River. Coordinates: 5.1697° N, 5.9297° E.

LAGOS – The area of the metropolis of Lagos was so named in 1472 by Ruy de Sequeira of Portugal "Lago de Curamo." In 1914, Lagos became the capital of the British Colony and Protectorate of Nigeria. In 1976, sixteen years after Nigeria gained independence, the then Federal Military Government of Nigeria promulgated decree No. 6 on 4 February 1976, which initiated the removal of the Federal Capital from Lagos to Abuja. The relocation of the Nigerian capital was completed in the early eighties. Lagos remains the largest city in West Africa and Nigeria's commercial capital. Coordinates: 6.5244° N, 3.3792° E.

TORU-NDORO- Her husband's hometown. Toru-Ndoro is in Ekeremor Local Government in Bayelsa State, Nigeria. Coordinates: 5.0391° N, 5.5978° E.

PORT HARCOURT- is the capital and largest city in Rivers State, Nigeria. It is Nigeria's fifth most populous city after Lagos, Kano, Ibadan, and Benin City. It lies along the Bonny River and is in the Niger Delta. Per Wikipedia, historically, Port Harcourt was known as Obomuotu Country, within which a few other smaller areas were called Diobu or Igweocha (city). The area that became Port Harcourt in 1912 was before a farmland belonging to the people of Ikwerre. The then colonial administration of Nigeria created the port to export coal from the collieries of Enugu, located 243 kilometers north of Port Harcourt. It was linked by a railway called the Eastern Line, also built by the British. Coordinates: 4°49'27"N 7°2'1"E.

JOS- is a city in the north-central region of Nigeria. Historians claim that the original name of 'Gwosh' was wrongly pronounced as 'Jos' by the Hausa who settled on the site and turned it into a trading center. Jos is the administrative capital and largest city of Plateau State, which was created out of the then Benue-Plateau State on February 3, 1976, by the Murtala Mohammed Regime. Plateau State gets its name from the Jos Plateau, a mountainous area in the north of the state with stunning rock formations. Bare rocks are scattered across the grasslands which cover the plateau. The altitude ranges from around 1,200 meters (about 4000 feet) to a peak of 1,829 meters above sea level in the Shere Hills range near Jos. The Jos Plateau is the source of many rivers in northern Nigeria including the Kaduna, Gongola, Hadejia, and Yobe rivers. Coordinates: 9.8965° N, 8.8583° E.

IBADAN- is Nigeria's largest city by geographical area. At the time of Nigeria's independence in 1960, Ibadan was the country's largest and most populous city and the second most populous in Africa behind Cairo. Ibadan is in southwestern Nigeria. According to the literature, the creation of Ibadan was circumstantial. Historians say that the history of Ibadan had long been preserved through oral history, but, still, the record says it came into existence in 1829 during a period of turmoil that characterized Yorubaland at the time. After the collapse of the Yoruba Empire at the end of the 18th century, 'Eba Odan', the phrase from which Ibadan is coined, had been populated by Yoruba rebels. 'Eba Odan' means in Yoruba between the forests and the plains, or literally 'by the edge of the meadow'. Seven hills surrounded it, and it functioned as a sacred area for the fighters that fled the wars. Ibadan is a prominent transit point between the coastal region and places in the hinterland of Nigeria. It had been the administrative center of the old Western Region since the early days of British colonial rule, and parts of the city's ancient protective walls still stand today. Coordinates: 7.3775° N, 3.9470° E.

KAINJI – The area around Kainji Lake is referred to as Kainji, and the lake supports irrigation and a local fishing industry. The Kainji Dam is a dam across the Niger River in Niger State located in central Nigeria. Construction of the dam began in 1964 to be completed in 1968. People were displaced by the construction of the dam and its reservoir, Kainji Lake, and were resettled by the Nigerian federal government. Coordinates: 10.3619° N, 4.6037° E.

ROTENBURG (WUEMME)- Rotenburg (Wuemme) is a town in Lower Saxony, Germany. It is the capital of the district of Rotenburg. Rotenburg is situated on the Wuemme river, which lies between the rivers Elbe and Weser at about the same latitude as Hamburg and Bremen, the latter lying 40 km to the west. It is often called "Rotenburg (Wuemme)" to distinguish it from
Rotenburg an der Fulda in the German state of Hesse and Rothenburg ob der Tauber in the German State of Bavaria. Coordinates: 53.1035° N, 9.3971° E.

YENAGOA - is a Local Government Area and the capital city of Bayelsa State, Nigeria. It is in the southern part of the country. The Izons form most of the state. Coordinates: 4°55′29″N 6°15′51″E.

My mother, in Lagos, Nigeria, circa 1973

Introduction

How this Story Came to Be Told

W hy have I written the story of my mother, and more importantly, why should you care to read it? After all, my mother is not Marie Curie, Oprah Winfrey, Miriam Makeba (nickname Mama Africa), Queen Elizabeth II, or the legendary warrior Queen Amina of Zaria. My mother is a retired eighty-four-year-old woman in the twilight of her life from the western Izon (Ijaw) tribe in the Niger Delta area of Nigeria. She currently resides in the comfort of her home in her riverine hometown of Ojobo. Ojobo is pronounced 'Ozobo' in the Izon language. Ancestry experts estimate that most of us would be forgotten four generations down the line or, as the Twitter handle Navalism put it in what I thought as a cynical but accurate tweet on November 10, 2022, "the reality is life is a single-player game. You're born alone. You're going to die alone. All your interpretations are alone. All your memories are alone. You're gone in three generations, and nobody cares. Before you showed up, nobody cared. It's all single player". For me, four generations were an overestimation; forgetting my ancestors started to occur before that timeline.

I am ashamed to say that in the writing of this story, I had to ask my mother what the names of her grandmothers were. I come from them, and I didn't know their names off the top of my head. And worse, that was just on my maternal side. I do not know the names of my paternal great-grandmothers or have any knowledge of them either. Sadly, I will never know as my father is no longer alive for me to ask. I only know my paternal great-grandfather's name because one of my distant cousins is named after him. I am not alone in this ignorance of who my ancestors are; after all, that is why companies like 'ancestry.com', 'FamilySearch.org', 'MyHeritage', and 'webtrees' are so profitable. Google has ancestry.com's 2015 revenue at US$683.1 million, making it apparent that people want to know from whom they come. I do not know anything about the algorithms companies like ancestry.com and others like it use to help people trace their ancestors. Still, I know they cannot help somebody like me despite the over seven billion genealogy records they claim to have because of where I come from.

My family information would not be in this database because no one would have put it in. And even if the data were there, it would only give me my ancestors' names, and I would still have the desire to know who they were; who and what they loved; what their fears and joys were, and the algorithm would not be able to fulfill this desire. It's no different from walking through a graveyard and seeing names on headstones. Nothing on a headstone tells you what made the person in the grave who they were. You only see their names, birth, and death dates. I call that *life statistics*. You see them through the eyes of others. You see descriptions like beloved daughter, friend, beloved son, beloved father, cherished mother, adored grandfather, etc. I believe we would all like to be known for what made us the persons we were rather than just our life's statistics. I would.

A dear friend of mine passed away a few months ago, in July 2022, at fifty from cancer. She texted me five months earlier to inform me about her grim diagnosis and thank me for our friendship. *Can you believe that*? She was dying, and she took the time to thank people for what they meant to her. What a remarkable person she was.

Nevertheless, I was expecting to hear about her death at any moment after our text exchange and had been trying to make my peace with it. She passed away on a hot summer day, and at her remembrance six days later; her husband talked about her profound sadness in her last days when she bemoaned that her future grandchildren, that were yet to be conceived, much less born, would never get to know her. That broke my heart more than her passing, and I have thought about how sad she must have been about this every day since. I knew her for ten years, and as life happens, I might move away or lose contact with her family for reasons beyond our control and never meet her future grandchildren and tell them about who I knew her to be. I will never forget her self-deprecating humor; that she liked Vietnamese food, particularly lemongrass chicken with rice vermicelli; or that she did not like to tell anyone when her birthday was so that no one would make a fuss.

This made me take stock. In doing so, I asked myself: what did I know about my parents as 'persons' that I could share with my adult children that they could later share with their children and grandchildren if they are so blessed? Have I shown my adult children who I am in my own right? Would they know enough about me, the person, to share with my yet-to-be-conceived grandchildren? I couldn't help but ponder how to answer these questions all the time. As I thought about these questions, two themes floated to the surface of my mind, giving me insights on tackling them. These themes later crystallized into two clauses in my head:

'Of whom we come, and whence we came.'

I promised myself I would explore them in depth to be able to answer the questions I was asking myself.

So, how did I go from exploring these two themes to telling my mother's story, you might ask? It started a few months earlier, on New Year's Day of 2022.

Eight days before New Year's Day 2022, we had topped up my mother's credit/ airtime on her mobile phone, so she could call us whenever she felt like it after being unable to contact us on her own a few months prior. On one of the first calls to me afterward, she asked if we could try to have daily calls whenever possible. I could tell from her voice that the months of being unable to talk to us directly for months had taken a toll on her. Her exact words were, "*I just want to hear your voice.*" As soon as she asked, I mentally checked my schedule to see if this would be feasible. I was going to try my best to make it work. You see, I have lived outside my home country Nigeria for the past twenty-six years, and our only means of communicating with each other is through the telephone. Since I left Nigeria in 1996, I have only been able to see my mother a total of seven multi-day/multi-month times, including her visiting me twice in Germany when I lived there and me returning to Nigeria to visit her and bury my father. I also realized that time was no longer on our side with my mother's age and mine.

The anxiety that my mother might get infected with COVID-19 was taking a toll on us as the vaccination regime in Bayelsa State, Nigeria was not as widespread as it was becoming in Canada and other countries. Between working remotely from home because of the pandemic and the seven-hour time difference between Nigeria and Calgary, Canada, where I live, I was able to move my schedule around. We agreed that we would try to have daily calls at 10 pm Nigerian time after she had watched her cable show for the day. We started having our daily calls on 16 January 2022. After a few weeks, we both realized that these daily calls made us happy. Through talking daily, we worried less about each other, laughed a lot, and began to build memories that will live in our hearts forever.

In our conversations, I found out things about my mother that I did not know, making me question how well I knew her as a person. I began to think, how well can you know the person who carried you for nine months, birthed you, and gave you life? When I became pregnant with my first child twenty-four years ago, I assumed (maybe naively) that the relationship between a mother and a child would be the 'closest' relationship possible. I know this is not the case, and as you and your child grow up together, that relationship can only be close if the mother works on it when the child is young, and the child joins her in that work when the child is old enough, and they are both willing.

The more we spoke, the more I learned about my mother. I learned about her past and present hopes, her dreams and fears, and her sufferings and joys. As time passed, I saw her personhood and what makes her who she was. Though we talk through video call technology connecting us over seven thousand miles apart, I understand the stories behind her facial expressions. The telephone's inner computer cannot learn these stories. Still, as she tells me about some defining moments of her life and shares one anecdote after the other, I see her humanity as clearly as I see mine. I define a person's humanity as their individuality, their uniqueness, their autonomy, their dignity, and their human rights. This captures how I started to see my mother as a person in her own right, not just as my mother or my father's wife; after all, she was not born in one of those roles. By seeing her personhood, I started to have a greater understanding of her and empathized with her. What harmed her in the past hurts me; her sufferings have become my sufferings, and her joys have become my joys. We have talked more than we ever did when I was growing up, and as I write her story, we still have not run out of things to talk about.

∞ ∞ ∞

In April 2022, our communication was further enhanced when her youngest half-brother (my young uncle) helped her install *WhatsApp*, and our daily phone calls became daily video calls. Through the screen of my iPhone, I see her excitement and sadness when we talk about different topics and see her underneath the mask of motherhood. Everything inside of me regrets not having had the opportunity to speak to my father and see what made him the person he was beyond being my father. I yearned to know more about my mother. I wanted to write down or record our conversations to capture the essence of who she is and transfer her spirit to my children and her other descendants.

Every time we spoke, I thought about this. After about two months, I gathered the courage to ask but was still anxious about how she would react. I asked her if I could question her about her childhood, how she grew up, and her life story to write these down for posterity. She said yes, of course. She was surprised and excited that I was interested in her life story, and our conversations became a collaboration of sorts. She was gratified that I wanted to know about the life she had lived and to share this with my children and others. What she did not know, and what I had not realized at the time, was the idea of interviewing her, so to speak, and writing down her answers and other anecdotes about her life that she was generous to share with me was a way to keep her alive and carry her with me as long as I live. This realization dawned on me months later when I was transcribing my notes from my interviews with her when I heard Kirsten Johnson (a filmmaker who had made a Netflix documentary about her father who had dementia - *Dick Johnson is Dead*) encapsulate precisely what I was feeling as she explained to Anderson Cooper what making this film about her father meant in one of the episodes of his podcast *All There is*. The episode is called *Anticipatory Grief*. "Reaching across time and space, being alive means we are carrying this multitude of people with us, and some of those people are our ancestors who did not get a chance to leave anything behind. No stuff, no creative work. They just survived, and somehow, they gave us life. Everyone carries a legacy that is rich, and yet there is less evidence of it, depending on who they are...."

There might be no evidence of my mother's life years after she is gone like all my ancestors before her, but if my telling her story in this book documents her legacy in some small way for me and those who come after me, she would have left something behind.

As Kirsten and Anderson further discussed in that conversation, I can confirm that asking my mother to share her life story was intimidating. It implicitly brought death into the equation, as they said it does in these situations. My mother and

I both knew without us saying it that I had asked to do this for when she would no longer be here. We are both aware that our limited time together is getting even shorter with our current ages. One thing I have always treasured about my parents in their conversations with me growing up was that they never shied away from talking about death. Death was ever present where they came from, so I believe it always accompanied them as they lived and live. My father tended to take it too far; every time he was ill, even with a slight cold, he would talk about his death like it was imminent. It used to freak us out. Now in retrospect, as I collaborate with my mother on this project and record her voice when I can't write as fast as we talk, I wish I had a recording of my father's voice to play for my children and their cousins. They only know him from what we share about him. My children can never hear what he sounded like. I still hear his boisterous and full laughter in my head, but the sound is getting fainter as the days go by and I grow older. As an adult, I have spent time with people who do not talk about death. The idea of talking to their children about the one inevitable thing in life is almost *verboten*. I have no idea why that is. As the character King T' Chaka in *Black Panther* said, "a parent who has not prepared her or his children for her or his death has failed as a parent." I agree.

∞∞∞

So, why I planned to write my mother's story was now clear to me; the next thing I had to tackle was how to write it. In 1976, the late Nigerian/ Cameroonian musician Nico Mbarga (known professionally as Prince Nico Mbarga), with his band Rocafil Jazz recorded a significant hit, '*Sweet Mother*,' which is the best-selling song in history by an African recording artist and recorded by an African label and it became and still is the anthem for how our mothers are seen and are expected to be. Sung in Pidgin English, it starts with these four lines:

Sweet mother, I no go forget you
For this suffer wey you suffer for me yé
Sweet mother, I no go forget you
For this suffer wey you suffer for me yé

The themes of suffering and doing everything for your child run through the entire song and encompass how a woman who has become a mother is defined in many cultures. The song portrays our mothers as just mothers and nothing else. But I ask, is that all there is in a mother? Shouldn't we separate the mother from the person, i.e., the human being? Becoming a mother twenty-three years ago and now a mother of adult children, I try to see myself not only through the optical prism of motherhood but also of personhood. I fail more times than I succeed when I do that, as both are intertwined once you become a mother, but I try.

Hence, I am letting the 'why' guide me to the 'how' I would do this. The 'how' I have come to see must be about capturing all that makes my mother who she is from her lips and perspective. This must be about her as a *'person'*: her fears, her joys, her loves, her hopes, and her dreams. It should not be about her as a wife, a mother, a grandmother, and, blessedly, a great-grandmother, as none of us is born already in those roles. We become them throughout life, but we start as individuals. It would also be presumptuous to address what my mother is to others as that would be from a perspective that is not hers.

In trying to formulate the 'how,' I came across a quote from an unknown person in one of those well-intentioned encouraging inspirational quotes that come up on *Momentum,* a Google Chrome Extension. It said, "on your journey through life, make sure your biography has at least one extraordinary chapter." It struck me that the quote does not instruct you on determining if your journey in life has an extraordinary chapter. I say you decide no matter who you are, as your story is yours. This is my mother's story, and I posit that all the chapters of her life have been extraordinary so far. Thus, I will tell her story as she narrates it to me, interspersed with some questions I asked her and her answers in her own words as hearing some parts of her story and how she tells it better captures her essence than my words ever could.

Chapter One

Childhood at Ojobo – A family of two: 1938-1950

My mother was born Lydia Brisibe on 2 June 1938, to her mother, Okpe, and father, Chief Francis Brisibe Adamagu, and a larger polygamous family in her hometown of Ojobo in present-day Delta State in Nigeria. Ojobo is located on the 'Boloutoru' creek in western Izonland and, at that time, was part of colonial Southern Nigeria before the division of the south of Nigeria into the Eastern and Western provinces in 1939. Our people, the Izon people or *'Izon Otu'* in our Izon language, are otherwise known as the Ijaw people due to the historic mispronunciation of the word Izon. We are an ethnic group majorly found in the Niger Delta in Nigeria.

My mother was born during the second world war. King George VI (the father of the recently deceased Queen Elizabeth the 2nd) was the King of England; Sir Bernard Henry Bourdillon was the colonial Governor-General of an amalgamated Nigeria; and according to the *Annual Report of the Colonies, Nigeria 1938*, published by the then English King George VI's Stationery Office (Nr. 1904) in 1939, the *Ijaws* were on the ten 'major' tribes in the colony of Nigeria and "seem never to have developed any political organization higher than that of the town or small group of villages".

Me: "Who named you Lydia? Do you know if it was your mother or father?"

My Mother: "Neither of them did. My mother told me that I was given the name Lydia by a tenant of my father who was a teacher living in my father's compound at the time."

Me: "How do you know your birth date when births were not recorded?"

My Mother: "My father recorded the birth dates of all his children. I don't know why he did that."

As an infant and young girl, my mother was the only child of her mother, and they were very close as, for all intents and purposes, they were a family of two and only had each other. Granny Okpe worked hard to provide for my mother and herself. In traditional Izon households, a mother is responsible for feeding her children and providing them with the necessities of life. Regarding her father, my mother says she had a healthy fear of him, like all children of that generation. My grandfather, Chief Francis Brisibe, was an important man with many wives and children in my mother's eyes and the eyes of everyone in that environment. It is estimated that he was born in 1894, which meant he was forty-four years old when my mother was born in 1938, so she fell into the category of his children born in the middle of his life.

My mother and Granny Okpe lived in a clay hut that my grandfather Chief Brisibe had assigned to Granny Okpe when he married her as one of his wives. She was one of my grandfather's 'senior' wives, or the wives he had married as a younger man. Four of the senior wives lived in clay huts attached. These huts were lined in a row not far from the main house where he lived. Granny Okpe and all the other senior wives have all passed away, but the huts they lived in are still there. Some have been rebuilt or renovated by their descendants.

Granny Okpe went fishing or farming daily except on market days. It was the tradition and an unspoken rule that no one went fishing or farming on market days, every eighth day. When her mother was away fishing or farming, my mother spent time at a fishing camp on the outskirts of Ojobo with her maternal grandmother Ebitoubo. Ebitoubo lived close to my grandfather's compound, so my mother did not have to go far to stay with her grandmother.

Me: "Did you enjoy spending time when you were young

and during your holidays in the fishing camp with your grandmother?"

My Mother: "I enjoyed spending time with my grandmother as she indulged me as her oldest grandchild who lived close by, but I did not enjoy spending time in the fishing camp. It felt dire and hopeless. I was terrified that I would grow older and never get a chance to go anywhere beyond my mother's hut and the fishing camp. I don't know why I felt that way at such a young age as I knew nothing else, but something in my gut kept telling me that there were other places in this world outside of what I was exposed to at that time."

My mother and granny Okpe would converse, cook, and eat together in their little hut after granny Okpe returned daily from the forest. On the other hand, as the head of a large family, her father never communicated with his young daughters unless he needed them to run errands, as far as she knew. My mother gladly ran errands and did chores for him as it made her feel important to serve her father; she told me he was an important man. For example, he would leave his laundry in front of his house, and she and her other half-sisters would take the initiative to wash his clothes and iron them. He expected them to do these without being told, and they did. My mother's half-sisters that were her peers included my late aunties Suwedé, Erébiri, Pinéré, and Yoémi.

My mother remembers she started elementary school when the measurement of either of her hands could go over her head and ears. That was how school-age eligibility was determined at that time. She was not yet literate, so she did not remember the day or the year. We are estimating by reversing the timeline from when she finished elementary school to a guesstimate of when she started.

Granny Okpe wanted my mother to be a small business trader and did not want her to follow in her footsteps in manual labor as a fisherwoman or a farmer. My granny worked every day when my mother was young except for the market days, and she did not want the same life path for her daughter. On the other hand, her father's wish was for her to attend school. At that time, all her half-sisters of her age did not attend school. Her father wanted her to attend school to reward granny Okpe for her obedience to him. Until she passed away in 2001, my granny was a quiet, diligent woman. My mother says she obeyed her husband without question throughout their marriage. She supported her husband in his trading business, and whenever he would ask her to go with him on his trade trips, she never complained and did all the physical work required of her to support his business. Therefore, letting my mother attend school was his reward to my granny. My mother puts it this way- "my father determined that I would one day 'become somebody,' i.e., 'Keme Pamini' in our Izon language". He did not say this because my mother was intelligent or hardworking, but because my granny Okpe was kind. He believed her kindness would be rewarded, with my mother, her only child at the time, becoming a person of substance in some way, shape, or form.

Becoming Literate, Fear Of A Wasted Life And Larcombe's Upper Standard

My mother attended the Native Administration Primary School at Ojobo from 1947 to 1953. That was what the school was called when she attended, as it was during colonial times. Today, the school is called Ojobo Primary School. She loved school and stated that she could passably read and write in 1950 when she was twelve years old. She saw attending school as a possible way out of the life she would have had to live for the rest of her days in Ojobo, which meant going to the forest daily to farm and fish. She did not want the traditional life of an Izon woman for herself as she saw it as a lifetime imprisonment of looking at the other side of the same river day-in-day-out. She was prepared to do anything to escape that path.

Me: "Why were you so terrified of never leaving Ojobo and living your entire life there?"

My Mother: "Before I started school, I had many sleepless nights of my life wasting away before my eyes if nothing changed. I have no idea why I felt that way. It was a constant feeling that got worse because some of my older half-brothers lived in urban areas and occasionally came to Ojobo to visit from their stations. I wanted to be like them and live that life so I could care for my mother. From them, I knew there was more to life than our creek and the villages like Ojobo along them. I was a naturally curious person, so I wanted to see more of what was out there. When I started school, some of our teachers were from other tribes close to the Izons. They were Urhobos and Itsekiris, making me more curious about where they came from and what their hometowns were like. It was my first exposure to non-Izon-speaking people, and they talked to us about places like Warri Township and Sapele".

My mother's favorite subject at school was arithmetic/ mathematics. Unlike most people of her age in Nigeria and generations after her, she enjoyed learning from the dreaded *Larcombe's Primary Mathematics (Metric Edition) Upper Standard Book*, the last mathematics textbook she used in primary school. She states that by the time she finished her primary school education in 1953 when she was fifteen years old, she had solved all the math problems in this textbook because she was interested in the subject.

This textbook has been and is still dreaded by primary school pupils in English-speaking West Africa. Many pupils found the math problems in this textbook difficult. I am sure if I scour the internet, I will come across a Facebook group or a group of people on another social media platform bemoaning their experiences with this textbook.

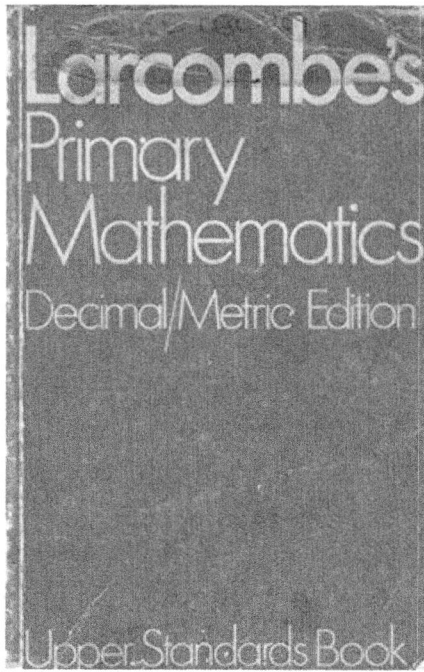

Taken from the Nairaland website (Image
may be subject to copyright)

I found this image above of the textbook on the internet, and I still shudder at seeing it. From my experience, when it was the recommended math textbook for me in primary five in 1976/1977, the math word problems in it were difficult to tackle. Still, my mother mastered them, and many years later, as a mother to young children, she helped us with our homework tackling these problems.

As a child, you assume your parents know everything, and to a certain extent, you believe they have all the answers. Because my mother bore the brunt of helping us with our math homework when I was in primary school, I presumed she had gained the knowledge she shared with us from a grammar school education. As I grew older, this presumption was cemented as I observed her manage her various small businesses and do mental calculations on large numbers that she can still conduct at her age of eighty-four. This skillset she has amazes me, as my brain isn't nearly as well-tailored for math.

Years later, when I became a mother and my mother visited me in Germany, she spent many hours studying fairy tale stories like *Tom Thumb*, *Thumbelina*, and *Little Red Riding Hood* from the Penguin Imprint *Ladybird Books for Toddlers and Young Children*, to read to my infant children. So, I was stunned when I was interviewing her during this collaborative project about her time in school when she told me that the extent of her schooling was only a primary school education that ended in 1953.

How did I not know that all these years?

My mother is business-savvy, and you will see this as I continue to tell her story in this book. I was speechless for about a minute, and she laughed at my shock as she thought I knew. I realized then that she was self-taught, and she continues to learn every day.

∞ ∞ ∞

1950-No Longer An Only Child

1950 was challenging for my mother as Granny Okpe became pregnant and gave birth to her only full sibling. She was terrified throughout her mother's pregnancy, as maternal mortality was commonplace. As an only child, she only had her mother and was scared that if her mother died during pregnancy or childbirth, she would be all alone. Fortunately, that did not happen, and her sister Susannah was born in 1950 when my mother was twelve years old, and they became a small family of three within their larger polygamous family.

Chapter Three

Arranged Marriage: 1956

From Fifteen To Eighteen Years Old

At fifteen, my mother completed her primary school education. Between the ages of fifteen and eighteen, she spent all her time helping her mother. She saw her male half-siblings doing all sorts of manual labor for their mothers, and she did not want her mother to feel that she was less because she did not have a son, so she tried to do for her mother all that her half-brothers did for their mothers. She went to the farm daily with her mother and worked alongside her. She also, during that period, worked with Ebitoubo in the fishing camps. Sometimes, her mother would send my mother to her maternal uncle Elakemfa, who lived in her maternal grandmother's hometown of Bomadi. Bomadi was a town, unlike Ojobo, which was a village. Elakemfa's mother and Ebitoubo were sisters, so he was Granny Okpe's first cousin. Elakemfa was a trader, so my mother enjoyed visiting with him and his family and working for him as he traded down their creek and along the Forcados River. Spending time with Elakemfa gave her a chance to travel and see other places.

My mother was seventeen at the turn of the new year in 1956. She had been of *marriageable* age for a while by the standards of that time, so she was not surprised when her father sent for her and told her that he had arranged a marriage for her with a man in the Nigerian capital city of Lagos. Granny Okpe married at fifteen, which was par for the course then in the rural areas of Nigeria. Unfortunately, this is still common in today's

Northern Nigeria.

So, who was this man that my mother was supposed to marry? Short answer, this man turned out to be my father, but there was a history behind why my grandfather Brisibe chose him and not anybody else as my mother's groom. I only know part of the history, which is the part known to my mother that she had previously shared with me and expanded on during our collaboration. I think the history is fascinating as it upended my views of the relationships possible between men and women in my grandparents' era.

My grandfather Brisibe took many wives during his life. One of those wives was a woman called Sasi, who was my father's half-sister. They were born to the same mother, a woman named Enaitoru (my paternal grandmother), but were of different fathers. My grandmother Enaitoru bore two children to Sasi's father and after he passed away, she was given to my paternal grandfather Atte as part of the Izon death rites.

How you might ask, did one of my mother's stepmothers become her sister-in-law? My head spun when I heard this history for the first time. My grandfather Brisibe and my aunty Sasi were briefly married, and in their brief marriage, they had five sons together, who sadly all died as infants. My grandmother Enaitoru liked having my grandfather Brisibe as her son-in-law during his marriage with her daughter. My mother shared that people who lived during that time said she was very upset when Sasi left my grandfather. She had seen how well the sons he had borne with other women were thriving, and she wanted grandsons of the same ilk. So, she was despondent that none of her grandsons from that marriage had survived infancy and grown up to be like their older paternal half-brothers. I cannot stop imagining that if one or all of them had survived, they would have simultaneously been my mother's half-brothers, her husband's nephews, and my uncles and cousins. Maybe, my parents would never have married? I digress. Back to the history.

My grandmother Enaitoru passed away in 1950 from

cerebral malaria, but my grandfather Brisibe still had a fondness for his former mother-in-law as they became friends. According to my mother, he respected her because she was a woman of principle. After Sasi left him, he kept in touch with her as she lived in her hometown of Peretoru, not far from Ojobo. He knew of her wish for their families to be connected by marriage. So, when he became aware of Enaitoru's youngest son, my father, who was single and living in Lagos, he thought giving him one of his daughters in marriage would be an excellent way to respect his friend Enaitoru's wish to connect their families.

Me: "What did you think when your father told you, you were going to marry a man you had never met and that he lived in Lagos? What did you say?"

My Mother: "I did not object as I thought my father would not suggest something that would be bad for me."

Me: "You trusted his judgment just like that? What did granny say?"

My Mother: "I thought I would survive no matter the circumstances of the marriage. I went to the forest every day with my mother, and I was always afraid that would be all I would do until I married a man in Ojobo or another Izon village, continuing the same hard life. My father had told me that my husband-to-be was young and single, and there was nothing wrong with him physically. It meant I would leave Ojobo for Lagos with a chance for a better life, I hoped. I had previously been to Warri with my father when he was trading and doing motorboat transport business. I had heard about Lagos from my half-brothers and that it was Nigeria's center of commercial activities."

Me: "So Granny said nothing?"

My Mother: "What could she say? As you know, women had no say in such matters, especially when my father had made the decision. All my older half-brothers involved in the decision supported the idea, which sealed it for me. My mother accepted the decision like I did as she also thought my father would not suggest something that would be bad for me."

Me: "What else did you think of the prospect of marrying someone you had never met?"

My Mother: "My only thoughts were, what would he look like and what kind of person would he be? I hoped he was not going to be lazy or a drunkard. As far as I was concerned, if he were not blind or bedridden, I would marry him and make the best of the marriage."

I closed my notebook to digest what my mother had just said. She asked me if I was okay as I was quiet after she answered my last question. We said our goodbyes for that day, and I couldn't stop thinking about how she must have felt at the thought of plunging into the unknown of marriage to a stranger. I knew my grandfather Brisibe had arranged my parents' marriage, but I had never thought about how it came about and what she thought when she agreed. She was fortunate that he was not a serial killer or a physical abuser, or some other type of monster.

∞∞∞

Leaving Ojobo For Hopefully A Better Life

After she agreed to the marriage and became betrothed, my father's cousins, her future in-laws, transported her first to Peretoru, his mother's hometown, where he had gone to school and lived before he moved to Lagos. She was familiar with Peretoru as it was also her mother's hometown and she visited it often to see her maternal cousins. From there, they took her to Lagos, and she left the Boloutoru creek, her mother and sister, and the life she knew for a new life, hoping it would be a better life.

Chapter Four

Double Deck Marriage and Early Married Life in Lagos: 1956 – 1960

The new Queen of England visiting Nigeria in 1956 and the 1956–57 Nigerian regional elections were the two significant events that happened in Nigeria in 1956. For my mother, the most significant event of 1956 was her marrying my father in an Izon traditional customary ceremony on April 24.

Their marriage became a *Double-Deck Marriage* when they married under the Nigerian *Marriage Act* two years later. What is a Double-Deck Marriage, you might ask? Simply defined, a Double-Deck Marriage is a celebration by the same couple who marry under one system and subsequently marry under another system. The most prominent of Double-Deck marriages in Nigeria is the celebration of customary marriage under traditional customary law before the celebration of statutory marriage, which is, marriage under the *Marriage Act*. This is what my parents did. They first had the customary traditional Izon marriage ceremony. My mother's half-brothers F.H.E Brisibe, J.D. Brisibe, Egina Brisibe, Custom Brisibe, and her first cousin John M. Zuokumor represented her extended family at this ceremony. She was still seventeen and six weeks shy of her eighteenth birthday. Two years later, my parents married legally under the Marriage Act in the Jehovah's Witness Kingdom Hall they attended in front of 'Witnesses'.

I find the Double-Deck Marriage system interesting. When I reviewed it to incorporate it to tell my mother's story, I realized neither my mother nor father understood its validity and what was precluded per the Marriage Act, especially with both of them coming from Izon polygamous backgrounds. Generally, the law forbids a man to contract another marriage either under the Act or under customary law with a third party while in possession of a valid Act marriage. As a result, a man will be subsequently guilty of bigamy if a couple already married under the Act goes thereafter to contract a customary marriage with a third party while still in possession of a valid statutory law marriage. It should be noted with much regret that this statutory provision has been violated by many people with impunity in Nigeria, depending on whom you ask. My mother says they got married in their Kingdom Hall as persons who came into the 'New World Society' but had not been married by the religious ceremonies of any of the authorized religions, so their marriage would be recognized by Jehovah's witnesses as binding and still having effect. Their marriage certificate from the legal ceremony is one of the few documents my mother still has in her possession.

Some Nigerian legal scholars, like Professor Itse Sagay, state that this does not mean that one can act with liberty when a marriage has been entered into under customary law. Marriage under customary law, they also say, can be dissolved on the following grounds:

1. Betrothal under marriageable age (*There is no fixed minimum age of marriage in customary laws. However, most systems do not permit marriage before puberty.*)
2. Refusal to consummate the marriage.
3. Harmful diseases of a permanent nature that may impair a woman's fertility or a man's virility.
4. Impotence of a husband or the sterility of a wife. (*I wonder who determines that a man is impotent, or a woman is sterile. Is it a doctor?*)
5. Conviction of either party for a crime involving a sentence of imprisonment of five years or more.
6. Ill-treatment, cruelty, or neglect of either party by the other.

7. Venereal disease contracted by either party. (*What if one party infects the other?*)
8. Lunacy of either party for three years or more. (*Lunacy?*)
9. Adultery. (*This ground is laughable, as a couple who had performed customary law marriage can subsequently perform a customary law marriage. The second marriage remains valid as customary law marriage by nature is polygamous and thus permits a man to marry as many wives as he wants.*)
10. Leprosy contracted by either party.
11. Desertion for a period of two years or more.
12. Lack of respect by the wife for the husband. (*What about lack of respect by the husband for the wife?*)
13. The man's inability to maintain the woman.
14. The use of charms or *juju*.
15. Engagement in witchcraft.
16. The wife's inability to cook.
17. Disgraceful and scandalous conduct on the part of the wife. (*What happens when the disgraceful and scandalous conduct is on the part of the husband?*)

The First Time She Saw Her Betrothed

As interesting as it was to find out that the common practice of celebrating a traditional marriage and, subsequently, a civil marriage under the *Marriage Act* in Nigeria is called a Double-Deck marriage, I could hardly wait to hear what my mother thought of my father the first time she saw him. After all, these are my parents, and the occasion is the first time they met. Wouldn't you be curious if it were your parents? We all tend to romanticize our parents' relationship no matter how far from romantic it is or was.

Me: "So, what did you think of Daddy the first time you saw him?."

My Mother: "When we arrived in Lagos, his cousins took me to his uncle Yaro's house in the then Marine Quarters neighborhood in Apapa, Lagos, to meet him. Yaro was his mother's half-brother. Shortly after we arrived, Yaro's wives prepared food for me to eat, and while I was waiting in their living room, your father came and stood by the door."

Me "And, what did you think of him?"

My Mother: "I was pleased that he was young like me and handsome. He was much better-looking than I expected."

I could feel her blushing as she answered me through the phone line. You know what I mean. Sometimes you can feel someone blushing without seeing them. You hear it through their voice on the telephone when you are discussing a topic that they might be embarrassed about or surprised about a topic you have brought up that they did not expect. My mother's generation doesn't talk about their love lives to their children. It is not common in my generation either. I have never shared with my children the exact details of how I felt when I met their father for the first time, and they have asked! It is deeply personal, so I understood my mother's reticence. She could not look me in the eye as we conversed through video, and I did not dare comment or chuckle. My mother was blushing! I did not press her anymore as I can imagine it was difficult for her to talk to me about her feelings about seeing the man she had been arranged to marry without first seeing him, despite it being my father. So, I waited for her to compose herself and changed the topic.

When my mother married my father, he lived in Ajegunle, a neighborhood located in the heart of Lagos. In the Yoruba language spoken in Lagos, Ajegunle means "a place where riches dwell". Many *Lagosians* have different views about Ajegunle. Some see it as a birthplace for criminals and prostitution. Others see it as a notorious slum, referring to it as the most disturbing ghetto in Nigeria. But Ajegunle is also noted to have produced notable personalities who have done well in their chosen careers. In 1956, when my father initially lived there, it was home to residents from almost all ethnic groups in Nigeria.

My father, in Lagos, Nigeria circa 1956-1965

Her First Marital Home-6 Igbobi Street, Apapa, Lagos

After their first marriage ceremony, my father's uncle Yaro suggested that the newlywed couple stay at one of my father's other uncles' places because my father's place in Ajegunle was small, and he had been having issues with his neighbors. Yaro felt it would not be safe for my mother to be there alone when my father was away at work. So, they stayed at my father's uncle

Otukpoki's house. Otukpoki was a sailor, so he was often away at sea for an extended period. My mother's first marital home address was thus 6 Igbobi Street, in the Marine Quarters Area of Apapa in Lagos. My mother says she enjoyed living there with her new husband, just the two of them. All their neighbors were Igbo-speaking from Eastern Nigeria; thus, my mother learned the language and the culture, living for the first time among another tribe. They lived in that little house in Marine Quarters for a while, and even after Otukpoki returned from his stint at sea, he looked for another place in Ajegunle and left them in his house in Marine Quarters.

When they got married in 1956, my father worked operating engines with the Nigerian Port Authority (NPA). His place of work was at the Apapa Wharf. According to my mother, this was temporary for him as he later studied and took the General Certificate of Education Ordinary Level Examinations (GCEs). He passed the exams and converted his job with the NPA to clerical accounting work. My mother took charge of their finances and saw that by the fifteenth of each month, they always ran out of money after paying their rent, their utility bills and buying groceries.

Me: "So what did you both do, seeing how tight things were for you financially?"

My Mother: "I became a small business trader. I sold everything sellable. When I started to trade, our money for feeding was no longer a problem. We kept his salary for our major expenses and used what I made from trading to cover groceries and other living expenses. We did not stop there; your father was also doing extra work."

Me: "Like what?"

My Mother: "Your father fished at the Apapa Quays every day after work, and I would clean and sell the fish he caught. It was hard work. It was dark by the time he got back from work, and he would go to the quays under the bridge with a torchlight and a spear. He was prolific and caught many fish.

∞ ∞ ∞

White Garment Church- Disagreement About Religion

My father was part of what we call in Nigeria a 'White Garment' church when my mother arrived in Lagos and married him. Members of these churches wear white garments as a form of uniform, and my research on this indicates that they do this because garments such as these were what they believed Christ wore during his suffering, crucifixion, and resurrection. My mother says the white garment church he attended was the 'Cherubim and Seraphim' church not far from where they lived.

On the first Sunday after they married, my mother was stunned to see her new husband put on his white garment that covered his entire body to his feet, for them to go to church. She had never seen this type of garment for worship as these white garment churches did not exist in or near Ojobo at the time. Though shocked, she took it in stride and went to church with him not knowing what to expect. She was not religious, and at Ojobo, when she went to church, she attended the Catholic church. When they got to the church, she saw that he was the band leader and a church worker.

Me: "What did you think about the service, the white garment, and the fact that they go barefoot?"

My Mother: "The white garment was surprising but not bothersome. The type of church and the service were foreign to me. No one in my family that I knew of was part of a church like that and I did not want to be the first. Also, I observed some things in the church that did not sit well with me."

Me: "Like what things?"

My Mother: "Your father asked me the same question when I

told him after we left the church that afternoon. I told your father that some of what went on in the service looked 'demonic' to me, and I would not be returning."

Me: "What did he say?"

My Mother: "He was not happy, but he said he would not force me to go with him."

After this point, he went with his friends, and my mother stayed home.

Me: "How did you manage as a couple with him going to his church with his friends and you staying at home? Did this cause any friction between you?"

My Mother: "Your father was not okay with what I had said about what I observed, but a few weeks later, the head of that particular church (the 'Aladura') confessed to some reprehensible acts."

Me: "What!"

My Mother: "Yes. Your father came home one Sunday after the service and told me, but he did not tell me the details of the acts. He just said he was not returning to the church, and he threw away his white garment."

My mother narrates that they fell into a timespan where they did not go to any church, but shortly after that, she drew my father's attention to some neighbors (a couple) who lived close by. She liked their lifestyle, mainly how they interacted with one another and their children. They later found out that the family was Jehovah's Witnesses. For that reason, they decided to also go to their neighbors' place of worship, the Jehovah's Witness Kingdom Hall in Apapa.

Fertility Issues And Conceiving Children

My mother says they did not conceive a child in the first three years of their marriage. According to her, they were both distraught, and as is the Izon custom, my father suggested she see an Izon native *'belly massager'* in Ajegunle. She refused as she did not trust that they knew what they were doing. She said if she had to go see native belly massagers, she would prefer to go back to her hometown of Ojobo, as she knew those who practiced their craft there. They went back and forth on what they should do and after much discussion, they decided to first go see a medical doctor. The next day, they went to a doctor at a private hospital called 'Lagoon Hospital'. Lagoon Hospital is still located on Liverpool Road in Apapa, Lagos. The doctor's services were expensive, my mother recalls, but they didn't care and used their savings to cover the expenses.

Me: "How was the appointment?"

My Mother: "The doctor was a white man, and it was my first time meeting a Caucasian. Your father had some Caucasians at his place of work in NPA. The doctor recommended testing me first as your father and I assumed that I had the fertility problems that prevented us from conceiving, after all, when a woman does not get pregnant where we came from, the woman was blamed. And as men always had many wives depending on their stature, all fertility problems are attributed to the woman."

Me: "It is not so different today."

My Mother: "Unfortunately, it is not."

Me: "Were you scared?"

My Mother: "I was terrified. If I could not get pregnant, your father could say he did not want to be married to me anymore and send me back to Ojobo and neither I nor anyone else would blame him."

The doctor found nothing wrong with my mother in all the tests he conducted. Then he told them, he wanted to test my father.

Me: "Were you surprised when he found nothing wrong in your tests and said he wanted to test your husband?"

My Mother: "I was shocked. Your father did not resist the testing to give him credit. Most men at that time would never have entertained the idea that they needed to be tested, much less that our fertility issues could be attributed to them. We both trusted the doctor and felt we were in good hands."

Me: "Why was that?"

My Mother: "He was respectful and came across as competent to us."

The tests on my father came back and showed a low sperm count. The doctor recommended medication that was then imported from England. When the medication arrived a few weeks later, according to my mother, he started to take one daily under the tongue, and a few months later, their first child was conceived. My mother went on to bear five children from 1961 to 1972.

Hearing from my mother that my parents and not just my mother suffered through infertility struggles made me think about how black women often cope with infertility alone. In Nigeria, this is often the norm then and now. Sadly, this problem is not limited to geography, as black women across the globe today often cope with this traumatic issue in silence and isolation. A 2015 University of Michigan study titled *'Silent and Infertile: An Intersectional Analysis of the Experiences of Socioeconomically Diverse African American Women with Infertility'* by Rosario Ceballo and her colleagues Erin Graham and Jamie Hart, reported on the findings from interviewing fifty African-American women of different socioeconomic backgrounds about infertility and relationships with friends, relatives, and doctors. Their respondents ranged from twenty-one to fifty-two, and most were married. Many of the women had college degrees and worked full-time.

In describing the difficulties of getting pregnant, the study showed that thirty-two percent of the women discussed stereotyped beliefs that equated being a woman with motherhood. This stereotyped belief is universal among many black women across the world. A quote from the study from some of the responses included: "Emotionally, I felt that I was not complete because I had not had a child. I didn't feel like I was a complete woman."

The study also showed that infertility was infused with religious significance for some of the women. The author of the study stated that the women believed God intended women to produce children, which further heightened their sense of shame.

The study further found that virtually all the women dealt with infertility in silence and isolation, even when a friend or relative knew about the woman's difficulty conceiving. Respondents of the study, the study authors say, thought infertility was not as emotionally painful for their husbands and partners, *who were not interviewed for the study*.

The researchers also noted that some women, especially those with secondary infertility, stayed silent about being unable to conceive because discussing it did not elicit sympathy or empathy. "Women may also reason that other people can neither change their infertility status nor understand what they were experiencing," Ceballo said.

Another commonality between black women in Nigeria and black women in the United States in this regard is that other reasons for women's silence about infertility may have to do with cultural expectations about strong, self-reliant black women who can cope with all adversity on their own and with notions about maintaining privacy in their communities. Ceballo also noted that she found that in the interviews, for example, respondents said, "You don't want people in your business" and "I never said anything to anyone else because in our culture…it was not something that you shared."

The study also found that about twenty-six percent of the respondents' interactions with doctors and medical professionals believed that encounters might have been influenced by gender, race, and/or class discrimination. The women talked about doctors who made assumptions about their sexual promiscuity and inability to pay for services or support a child.

The fact that in 1959/60 Lagos, in colonial Nigeria, my parents got competent fertility care, and in 2022, race-related disparities in fertility and maternal health are still prevalent among Black women is jarring. These inequalities are particularly resistant to change. Black, Indigenous, and People of Color (BIPOC) continue to have higher rates of infertility and lower rates of accessing fertility care than their white contemporaries—as well as a higher risk of maternal mortality, which is a major problem BIPOC women face to this day.

Chapter Five

The Nigeria Biafra Civil War: 1967-1970

From Being Married To An Aspiring Accountant To Becoming A Soldier's Wife

1961 to 1967 passed by fast for my mother as a mother of young children as it does for many young mothers. She had given birth to two children in this time span and was pregnant with a third that turned out to be me. Her husband was still working at NPA and had taken and passed some accounting designation examinations. He was climbing the corporate accounting ladder at NPA. Meanwhile, in Nigeria, there was a lot of turmoil and political uprisings at that time.

Nigeria gained independence from Britain in 1960 and by 1963 severed its remaining ties to Britain, marking the birth of the Nigerian First Republic. Three years later, on 15 January 1966, a military coup deposed the government of the First Republic, and many leading politicians of the First Republic were assassinated including Prime Minister Abubakar Tafawa Balewa, Premier of Northern Nigeria Ahmadu Bello, and Finance Minister Festus Okotie-Eboh. On 16 January 1966, the Federal Military Government of Nigeria was formed, with General Johnson Aguiyi-Ironsi acting as head of state and Supreme Commander of the Federal Republic of Nigeria. Six months later, on 29 July 1966, a countercoup by military officers from northern Nigeria deposed the Federal Military Government. Aguiyi-Ironsi and other senior southern military officers were assassinated and General Yakubu Gowon from northern Nigeria became Head of State.

The following year, in 1967, killings of people of Eastern Nigerian origin claimed the lives of many thousands, mostly Christian Igbo people. Historians say this was carried out by the Muslim Hausa and Fula people triggering a migration of many Igbos back to their hometowns in Eastern Nigeria. On 27 May 1967, Gowon announced further subdivision of Nigeria, into twelve states. These included the subdivision of the Eastern Region. Three days later, on 30 May 1967, General Chukwuemeka Odumegwu Ojukwu, Military Governor of Eastern Nigeria, declared his province an independent republic called Biafra and the Nigerian Biafra Civil War broke out.

My mother and her young family were not affected by the onset of the war as they lived in Lagos and, according to her, were a bit far from the war front. However, shortly afterward, as my mother tells it, my father traveled to his hometown Ndoro on leave and something traumatic happened to him at a military checkpoint on his journey back to Lagos. He narrated his ordeal to her upon his return. She said he felt humiliated and annoyed at how the soldiers at the checkpoint treated him. He concluded by telling her that he was going to join the Nigerian Army because he never wanted to feel the way he felt ever again. My mother was against it; she was worried that he could die, and she would be left alone with two young kids and a third that would arrive the following year. He joined the army despite her objections, insisting that he would be fine. My father was put in the Nigerian Army Pay Corps because of his accounting background but was still sent to the war front and there he saw combat. He was deployed to various places in the territories held by the Nigerian Army, but he was in a serious car accident on the way to his last deployment and suffered gruesome injuries: breaking his neck and his legs. My mother recalls that the army informed her after he was taken to the nearest military hospital.

After almost three years of civil war, on 8 January 1970, General Ojukwu fled into exile. His deputy Philip Effiong became acting President of Biafra and on 15 January 1970, Effiong surrendered to Nigerian forces and Biafra was reintegrated into

Nigeria.

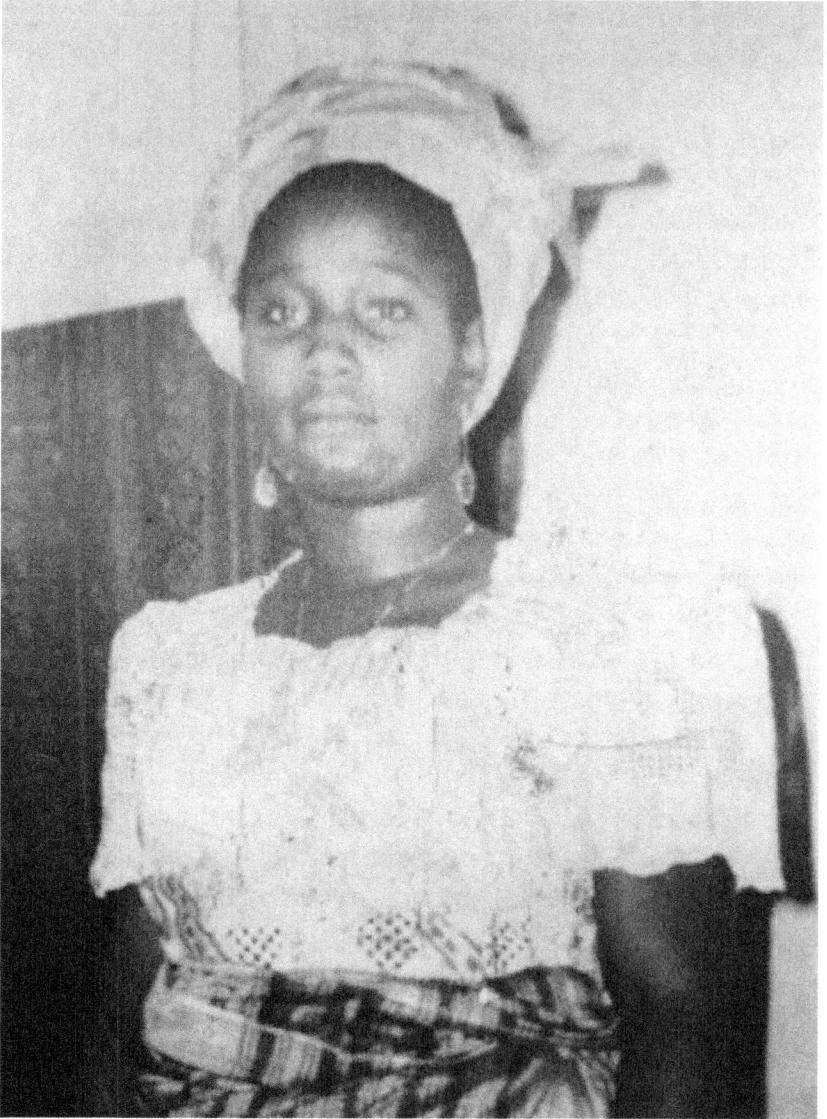

My mother, in Lagos, Nigeria, circa 1965.

Money Difficulties And The Start Of Their Polygamous Marriage

One day in late 1968 during the civil war, and my father was stationed in Lagos, my mother with three children from the ages of six months to seven years old to take care of, got a rude awakening when some of my father's relatives came to their small 'face-me-I face-you' residence at 68 Ojo Road in Apapa, Lagos. My mother was surprised that they had a young woman in tow who turned out to be the woman my father had taken as his second wife.

Me: "So you were not aware that he had taken a second wife?"

My Mother: "I was unaware. He never mentioned it. I did not know why they had come in such a large number, but when I saw that they were with a young woman that I did not recognize, I realized what was going on."

Me: "What did you say? What did you do?"

My Mother: "What could I say? What could I do? Polygamy is normal where we come from. My father, your paternal grandfather and all the men in our villages had many wives. I was a little bit sad that he did not warn me, not that I could have done anything about it. But I was worried about how we would manage financially. We already had three children, with the oldest in primary school and the second about to start nursery school. I worried about how we would pay school fees. Because of the civil war, things were difficult, and we were living solely on his military salary. I could not trade anymore as my customers were Igbo women, who had gone back to the East after the war broke out." The marriage between my father and his second wife did not last long.It lasted only six months and another six months later, he took a third wife. Five months after the war ended in 1970, my mother gave bith to her fourth child.

Chapter Six

Problems Abound in The Year of Our Lord 1972

After the war ended, my mother resumed trading after she organized childcare with one of her female relatives from Ojobo. My father had recovered from his car accident and financially, they were doing better. From the end of 1970 to early 1972, they saved enough to build their first house at 13 Iya Ojo Street in Ajegunle, Apapa Lagos. They built a bungalow that combined their living space with space to earn rental income. The house had a long corridor down the middle with eight rooms on each side of the corridor. They kept the first four rooms on the right for their family and rented out the remaining twelve rooms. There were four communal kitchens shared by the tenants and one kitchen that they kept for themselves. There were also four latrines at the back.

Things went south after my mother bore her fifth and last child and 1972 according to my mother, became the worst year of her life up to that point.

Illness & Loss; Detention & Court Martial

My grandfather Brisibe fell ill in mid-1972 and his prognosis was not good. Shortly afterward one afternoon in August of 1972, military policemen came by the house to talk to my father, asking him to report to their station forthwith. He told them he would report himself the following day at their station. They agreed and left. However, they returned a few hours later that night and arrested my father and one of my parents' tenants,

Sergeant 'Angelwire', who was my father's subordinate at his place of work.

I knew pieces of what had happened in that awful time for my parents, but this was the first time my mother was sharing a first-hand account of the events, the players involved, how this affected her, and how they survived this as a couple and a family.

Me: "How did you react when the military police with their red berets showed up at your house that afternoon?"

My Mother: "I was scared! What would I do on my own with five young children and one that was just two months old? How would we survive? Your father was calm because he knew he had done nothing wrong, and I will give you some background on why he felt that way. Your father believed everything would be cleared up once he went in the next day to answer their questions as they agreed to let him come in the next day. He kept reassuring me, but I was still terrified."

Me: "You must have lost your mind when they came back that night to arrest him and your tenant. What happened that made them come back that night to arrest him and your tenant?"

My Mother: "It was a terrifying sight when they came back that night and I am glad none of you was old enough to understand what was going on. They came in three army Land Rover vehicles with guns and lights blazing. The whole street knew something was amiss. They made your father and Angelwire dress in their uniforms, then they handcuffed them and took them away."

Me: "Do you know why they came back that night?"

My Mother: "I don't know exactly, but after the ordeal was over, your father and I believed that the military investigators sent them back, maybe thinking we would destroy evidence."

Me: "What did you do after they arrested him?"

My Mother: "When your father was arrested, I thought we were finished."

I could see that it was difficult for her to recall that painful time, so I kept quiet and waited for her to continue when she was ready.

My Mother: "I ran to my brother, Awiki's house first thing the next morning to tell him what had happened. My brother was a major in the Nigerian Army Education Corps at that time."

My mother goes on to tell me how my father's detention played out, but she also shared the background of how all this trouble came about.

My parents had rented one of the living room and bedroom combos to Angelwire and his family in early 1972. Angelwire and my father were both in the Nigerian Army Pay Corps. Whilst my father was an officer and held the rank of a lieutenant, Angelwire was an enlisted soldier (referred to in Nigeria as *Other Rank*). According to my mother, the Angelwires were *"living big"* for a family of five that was renting two rooms in my parents' house. Both my parents wondered how they could afford their lifestyle. My mother says as they observed how the family lived, she advised my father to *"open his eyes, and find out what is going on"*, as they worked together in the same pay office. She had a bad feeling about what could be going on and was afraid my father could be caught up unknowingly in whatever it was. Her fears were justified when a few weeks after their discussion, Sergeant Angelwire approached my father about a *"ghost soldiers' scheme"* he and others at my father's workplace were running. The scheme involved putting names of dead and other soldiers who had left the army after the war on the payroll and their pay was then circumvented to the schemers' pockets.

You see, Sergeant Angelwire was the only other Izon person at my father's workplace and as his tenant and fellow Izon man, he approached my father to bring him into the scheme. My mother says my father was appalled and refused to participate in a scheme that was cheating the Nigerian Army of millions of *Naira*. Sergeant Angelwire and others kept trying to convince my father at his workplace and he kept turning them down, saying he was not a thief or a scammer.

Unbeknownst to them, army investigators had uncovered the fraudulent scheme and were investigating the entire pay office where my father worked. When they had enough proof, they dispatched the military police to round up everyone who worked in that pay office.

After my mother ran to her brother's house seeking his help to find out where my father had been taken, Uncle Awiki found out a few days that they were first detained in the hold in Ann Barracks (a military base in Lagos), but they were later taken to a POW camp where former Biafran soldiers had been detained during the war. Uncle Awiki instructed her not to see or speak to anyone without first clearing it with him. My mother says that he wanted to protect her from being accused as a co-conspirator, and he visited her every week throughout the ordeal.

Me: "How long was Daddy in detention and how did you cope?"

My Mother: "Your father was in detention for five months before he was court-martialed."

Me: "Court-martialed?"

My Mother: "Yes. But while your father was in detention, my father died."

My mother received news of her father's death in late November, 1972. He had passed away at the University of Benin Teaching Hospital in Benin-City on November 28, 1972.She tried to go see my father where he was being detained to let him know that she would not visit him for a few weeks because she was going to her father's burial. My mother said my father understood and urged her to go knowing that this was important to her. Her half-brothers who lived in Lagos on the other hand urged her to stay in Lagos and be by her husband's side.

Me: "So, your brothers were in short telling you to stand by your man like in the Tammy Wynette song?"

My Mother: "What?"

Me: "I am just teasing. It is a song by a country singer in America."

My mother stared at me in confusion through her phone screen and I realized that my attempt to lighten the mood had not worked.

Me: "Please forget it. You were saying?"

My Mother: "I was not going to miss my father's burial. After much difficulty, I convinced my brothers why I had to go and pay my last respects to my father. I went to Ojobo for the burial and because some of my brothers were in the Nigerian Police Force at that time, they arranged for a police boat to take me back to Warri immediately after the burial, so I could return to my children and the situation with your father."

After the date of my father's court-martial was set for early 1973, my mother says that Uncle Awiki found out that the court-martial judge was going to be a certain Colonel Jallo. Uncle Awiki knew somebody who worked with Colonel Jallo and the person reassured them that Colonel Jallo was a fair man. By the time the court-martial began, my father's superior who had started the fraudulent scheme had been recalled from the United States where he was on course. He confessed to the entire scheme and stated that my father was innocent and was never part of the scheme. He said my father neither participated nor knew of the scheme until Sergeant Angelwire approached him. He also stated that he changed the payroll records after my father signed them for each month as he oversaw what my father approved before payment was made.

As a result, my father was cleared of all charges and immediately released. To give him a fresh start, the army transferred him to Port-Harcourt, the capital of Rivers State in the Niger Delta region of Nigeria. This was close to both my parents' hometowns. Sergeant Angelwire stayed in his post, and he did not serve any jail time because he was not the scheme's ringleader. My father's superior, the ringleader of the fraudulent scheme, was sentenced to jail time in military prison. The Angelwire family moved away after the court-martial and were no longer my parents' tenants.

Chapter Seven

Port-Harcourt: 1973-1974

Constant Financial Worries

When our family arrived in Port Harcourt in 1973, my mother did not know what to do for work. She was glad that they had left Lagos and the problems of the past year behind, but she also left behind her petty trader network where she earned her living. Things were even more difficult financially because my father had been detained without pay, and they were awaiting his back pay after he was exonerated. Nevertheless, they still had household expenditures to cover and boarding school fees for their first four children whom they had put in boarding school in Lagos, so our education would not be disrupted.

A few months of daily worrying went by, she narrates, and then one day, two friends of my father who were also army officers came by the house the army had provided for them in Port Harcourt to visit. As usual, when they came and she offered them refreshments, they would ask for *Stout Guinness*. My mother would have to organize getting them what they requested as she did not have any type of beer stocked in the house. That day, one of them asked her if she would be interested in selling beers and soft drinks (sodas for in North America) on a wholesale basis. He shared with her that he oversaw buying drinks in bulk for the army in Port-Harcourt at a controlled price. He encouraged her to gather all she had in cash as her capital and invest it by buying the drinks, marking them up slightly and then selling them wholesale to retailers.

Me: "What did you think when he told you this?"

My Mother: "I was overjoyed. I had been worrying constantly about how we would manage, so this was like God had heard my prayers. We were stretching your father's salary as far as we could, and it was not enough."

She gathered all her money and gave it to him. The next day, she took delivery of a truck full of drinks bought at the control price. She sold it at wholesale prices and made a sizable return on her investment. She was encouraged, and she then asked Effiong Akpan, her house help, to go to the market to do some recce work. He did, and then they both went back to talk to some of the retailers in the market, letting them know she would sell the drinks to them at a specific wholesale price. She was immediately inundated with customers. It was so busy that Effiong could not take his usual weekly day off. She compensated him and was relieved from her financial worries.

Good While It Lasted

My father took a fourth wife at the end of 1973 and by this time, my mother says it was par for the course. She focused on the well-being of her children and making sure the family could in her words *"more than float financially"*. This all came crashing down when my father came home one day from work and informed her that the army had transferred him to Jos, in today's Plateau State in Nigeria. The transfer to Port Harcourt lasted a year and according to my mother, it was a profitable one for her and the family, enabling her to pay her children's boarding and tuition fees as well as their flights to and from Lagos to Port Harcourt for the long holidays.

When my father informed her of the transfer to Jos, she initially considered staying put in Port Harcourt to continue her profitable wholesale drinks business, but she quickly realized she had no choice, so she packed up and moved to Jos with returned trepidation about how they would augment his military salary and take care of their family.

Chapter Eight

Jos 1974-1975: Attempt to Sell Ògógóró

Our family's stint in Jos was a short one that lasted just a year. During that period, my mother again tried to find a means of living to cover what my father's salary did not. She lived with this constant worry that never abated. I had no inkling of the fear my mother lived with trying to make sure her family was surviving financially. Having been a mother for almost twenty-four years now, I can relate to her fear having lived it for a while. Hearing her talk about the persistent anxiety she lived with, counting every penny to ensure the family not only had necessities like food, shelter, and clothing, but enough for a great education for the children, for the care of her mother and other relatives who depended on her, and my father, takes me back to those times and wonder how she coped, without us the children knowing.

In an article published by the New York Times (NYT) Parenting Newsletter titled *"Why Women Do the Household Worrying"* on April 21, 2021, and updated on June 2, 2021, my mother's eighty-third birthday (I appreciate this quirk), the writer Jessica Grose talks about the "one thing that remains frustratingly uneven: the *mental load*, which is a mostly invisible combination of anxiety and planning that is part of parenting". She states that this issue is *pernicious*, and she relates how excited she was to read the work of Allison Daminger, a Ph.D. candidate in sociology and social policy at Harvard University. Ms. Grose talks about Ms. Daminger's paper in the American Sociological Review on this topic that breaks down the mental load — "cognitive labor," in sociological terms — into four parts: *anticipate, identify, decide, monitor.* In the paper, Ms. Grose relates that for the paper, Ms. Daminger "conducted in-depth discussions with 35 couples, and found that the two parts of the process that are most heavily imbalanced are "*anticipate*" and "*monitor*" — women do most of those steps. "*Identify*" and "*decide*" tend to be done by men and women jointly".

I found this imbalance intriguing and I cite this article here to connect the universality of my mother's fear and why she carried the burden of constantly worrying i.e., the 'mental load' to the same affliction women including me tend to suffer from.

Jos did not offer my mother any clear possibilities of what to do to earn a living, so she attempted to trade our Nigerian local gin called Ògógóró from 'Ogog', a Yoruba word. Ògógóró is usually distilled locally from fermented Raffia palm tree juice, where it is known as Nigeria's homebrew. According to Wikipedia, "today, there is a misconception that Ògógóró can be pure ethanol, but traditionally, it had to come from the palm tree and then be distilled from this source". "It is popular throughout West Africa and goes by many names. Other Nigerian epithets include Udi Ogagan, Agbagba Urhobo, as well OHMS (Our Home-Made Stuff), Iced Water, Push Me, I Push You, and Craze man in the bottle. The Ghanaian moonshine is referred to as akpeteshie."

My mother planned to sell this locally distilled gin to enlisted soldiers in the army barracks because she had heard from some other officers' wives that many soldiers buy it. The barracks were located approximately fifty kilometers from where our family lived in Jos. Unfortunately, my mother did not conduct a deep enough feasibility study like she would normally do and relied on hearsay regarding the prospective customers before she invested in ten drums of Ògógóró. A standard drum used for Ògógóró has an inside dimension of 572 millimeters (22.5 inches) diameter and 851 millimeters (33.5 inches) height. These dimensions yield a volume of about 218.7 liters (57.8 US gal; 48.1 imp gal), but they are commonly filled to about 200 liters. She drove to the barracks daily when the children were at school despite how dangerous the roads were, and she did not sell a single drop. She had not factored that many of the enlisted soldiers that were posted to Jos from all parts of northern Nigeria were Muslim and because of their religion, did not drink alcohol.

Chapter Nine

Moving to the City Built on Seven Hills-Ibadan: 1975

After a year in Jos, to my mother's relief, the Nigerian Army transferred my father from the Pay Corps office of the 3rd Armored Division of the Nigerian Army headquartered in Jos to the Pay Corps office of the 2nd Mechanized Division of the Nigerian Army located in Ibadan, the capital of Oyo State, Nigeria making Ibadan home for the next seven years. I am giving you these details of the different army divisions as this is how my mother describes them to me.

According to my mother, Ibadan felt different than any other place they had lived or had been stationed in by the army. In trying to understand why Ibadan felt different to her from the other places she had lived after she got married, I looked to the words of John Pepper Clark-Bekederemo, (1935-2020, known popularly as J.P. Clark) in his poem 'Ibadan' named after the city. Eons ago, like many students who took the subject 'Literature in English' in secondary school in Nigeria, I had to study this poem. J.P. Clark was a renowned Nigerian poet and writer of Izon origin, and he wrote this short poem in 1965 describing the ancient city where he had lived as a student while at 'The University of Ibadan' (or UI as we Nigerians call it). The poem goes as follows:

> *"Ibadan,*
> *running splash of rust*
> *and gold-flung and scattered*
> *among seven hills like broken*
> *china in the sun."*

When I read this quintain for the first time in 1979 whilst living in Ibadan, my only understanding of it as an eleven-year-old was that the city was sprawled with rust-colored rooftops and was spread around the seven hills that make up the foundation of the city, which are Oke Padre, Oke Ado, Oke Bola, Oke Mapo, Oke Are, Oke Sapati and Oke Mokola. *Oke* means hill in Yoruba, and I knew many of the hills and the surrounding neighborhoods named after them because at that time we were Ibadan residents. Today, over forty years later, I cannot say if J.P. Clark was extolling the city or criticizing it in the poem. Alb Miz in his poem analysis of Carl Sandburg's poem '*Chicago*' states that "knowing the historical background of a poem is more important for a reader to understand the poem's intricacies and mood of the poem". I came across this piece of advice recently when I was looking for anything that could help me analyze J.P. Clark's poem. Since trying to decipher J.P. Clark's words was not my goal, I left that exercise alone after finding the only analysis of the poem that brings me closer to understanding the intangibles of why and how Ibadan 'felt' different to my mother. The analysis, states that "the lyrical poem describes Ibadan in terms of its expansive but uneven terrain; the disparities between the old and the new sections of the city, the poor and the rich in the city".

My mother uses the commonly spoken language as the comparing factor between Ibadan and the previous places she had lived in after she got married. She opines that Lagos as the then capital of Nigeria and today still the commercial capital, attracts a diverse demography from all tribes of Nigeria, making it easier for anyone to fit in if they can communicate in Nigeria's *lingua franca*, English. Port Harcourt at the time she lived there and now, is dominated by coastal peoples, including the Ikwerre, Ogoni, and Izon among others, so English is commonly spoken there. The most widely spoken language in Jos is Hausa, and because of the high literacy rate in Jos, almost everyone speaks English. My mother on her part never felt comfortable or lived in Jos long enough to learn Hausa. Ibadan, though a cosmopolitan city with settlers migrating from different places, is predominantly Yoruba speaking. She only knew a few words of Yoruba when she got to Ibadan, but this did not faze her. She was open to learning the language and appreciated that Ibadan kept its heritage as an ancient city.

Thus, she jumped into learning all she could about the city. After a few months, she saw the advantages of what Ibadan could offer her and our family. The most important advantage Ibadan offered, she thought, was that it was an epicenter of educational opportunities in Nigeria starting with it being the host to Nigeria's premier higher institution of learning, UI. UI was established in 1948 as a college of the University of London and later converted into an autonomous university in 1962. At that time, some of her nephews were attending UI and my father also had two relatives that were a student and a lecturer respectively. Ibadan also possessed numerous public and private primary and secondary schools located in the city and its suburbs that would benefit her growing children.

Another important advantage Ibadan offered, my mother surmised, is that Ibadan was a sprawling urban center that had become a major point of bulk trade, which gave her business opportunities because of its central location and accessibility from the capital city of Lagos. The location and the importance of Ibadan as a point of trade were factors that had been major considerations in the choice of Ibadan as the headquarters of the Western Provinces (in 1939 during colonial rule), which ranged from the northernmost areas of Oyo State to Ekeremor, Bomadi, and Patani. These were Izon regions my mother was familiar with that had been transferred from the old Delta province in the Old Western region and later Mid-west to the old Rivers state and later Bayelsa, in the redistricting of Nigeria carried out shortly before the Nigerian Civil War.

Considering all these factors, my mother decided that Ibadan was a place she could center her family for a while even if the army, as expected, would transfer my father to another city.

She had seen that the constant moving of the children that were becoming prepubescent and teenage age, was taking a toll and did not bode well for their stability and educational journey. To sell her decision to my father, she says she highlighted the education factor as in their marriage up to that point, they had often talked about the importance of the children's education and how they would do their best to provide us the best opportunities that they could afford.

Fishmongering, Kainji, And Danger

Shortly upon arriving in Ibadan in mid-1975, my mother, after organizing us children into the schools that had so impressed her, began an informal feasibility study into what she could trade to augment her husband's salary and provide for her family. Unlike in Jos, she had choices and was still contemplating them, when one of her older half-brothers J.D. Brisibe came to visit her at Ibadan where he was attending a police conference. After visiting with my mother for a few days, as he was getting ready to leave, he invited her to come to visit him and his family where he was stationed with the Nigeria Police Office near Kainji in Northcentral Nigeria.

Me: "He invited you? That was nice of him."

My Mother: "J.D. knew that I liked to visit new places."

Me; "So what did you say to his invitation?"

My Mother: "I said yes, of course, as I had never been to that part of the country."

A few months later, she traveled to where her brother was stationed near Kainji to go see her brother and his family. His wife Agbebor showed her the sights when she arrived and took her to the market at the waterside at Kainji. She wanted to buy fish and there was a large variety of fish there for sale. Kainji itself, in addition to the Dam and the Lake named after it, is a small fishing community. My mother found that there were many types of fish there: big and medium-sized. She saw how big the river Niger was there. Because the Kainji Dam was constructed there starting in 1964 and then opened in 1968, one side of the river was low, and the other was high, making it easy for the fishermen and fisherwomen to fish. After her visit for a week, she returned to Ibadan with some fish that she had bought in Kainji.

The next day after she returned to Ibadan, Dr. Egberike, a family friend from the same hometown as my father came by to visit my parents. According to my mother, as she related to them how much fish she saw in Kainji, Dr. Egberike in turn told them about his plans to start a canteen business at the UI campus. He was a lecturer in the English department, so it would be something he would be able to secure a license to do. He asked if she would supply him with fish for the canteen. My mother agreed, ecstatic that she would have a ready buyer if she embarked on this fishmongering business.

Not waiting for Dr. Egberike, my mother used some of her capital to buy a freezer and other tools for the business and embarked on going to Kainji to buy and bring fish back to Ibadan for sale. Her able 2iC Effiong was by her side in Ibadan, and they used word of mouth to spread the word of her new venture. Customers rushed to buy, and they sold a lot of fish. Despite this success, she ran into a big snag of an electricity supply problem. Electricity in Ibadan supplied by the then National Electric Power Authority (*not* known fondly by Nigerians as NEPA), was becoming unstable and things got worse with the supply. My mother could not afford a generator to keep the fish fresh in the freezer. To add to the unstable electricity supply, when she traveled weekly with my father's army-assigned driver to Kainji, she encountered many fatal car accidents on the way and back. To exacerbate things, the army had sent my father to Indianapolis in the United States of America for a three-month training course. So, the combination of the danger on the road, the possibility of being involved in a serious car accident and leaving her children all alone scared her, and she decided to stop fishmongering.

∞ ∞ ∞

Learning To Drive

Just after our family arrived in Ibadan and my mother had sorted out all her children in different schools, she was faced with the dilemma of all of us now attending day schools as opposed to boarding schools and would require to be transported to and from school daily. Though the army had assigned a driver to my father who drove us to school, my father suggested that my mother learn how to drive since they had decided that Ibadan would be the family's home base and if there was an emergency, she could take us to school or pick us up.

Me: "When Daddy suggested you learn how to drive, how did you feel about it?"

My Mother: "I liked the idea. In Port Harcourt, and Jos, the army driver had driven me everywhere and I always had to plan around your father's schedule at his workplace. I had seen many women driving especially wives of your father's colleagues, so I wanted the independence of being able to drive myself.'

Me: "So, who taught you how to drive?"

My Mother: "Initially your father taught me on the weekends, but the lessons did not go well."

Me: "What do you mean? What happened?"

My Mother: "We argued a lot as he was correcting me at every turn. He was nervous."

We both chuckled.

Me: "I understand him. It happens to a lot of people when they try to teach their spouse, or their child to drive."

My Mother: "Yes, then we agreed that his army-assigned driver, Kunle will teach me for all our sakes."

We both laughed.

Me: "How did that go?"

My Mother: "That went well. Kunle could not yell at me as I was his boss's wife. He did not take it easy on me though. As soon as I mastered the basics of driving in our neighborhood in Bashorun, he took me to the busiest area in Ibadan- the Dugbe market, where there was a lot of traffic with many cars and drivers all trying to get to their destinations."

Me: "So it was baptism by fire?"

My Mother: "Yes, it was, and it helped. In about five weeks, I was a confident driver and passed the test for my license."

Until June 2018, Saudi Arabia was the only country in the world in which women were forbidden from driving motor vehicles. Women in Nigeria pre- and post-independence did not face the restrictions that these Saudi women faced. Nonetheless, it is not a given that a woman from my mother's cultural and educational background would have the right to be afforded the freedom and independence that driving would give her. She would not have the ability to walk into a driving school to take driving classes without the finances to pay for it. In addition, even if she learned how to drive, she would still need access to a car that she most likely could not afford on her own. If the family owned a car, it would be her husband's and she would need his permission to drive 'his' car.

Overcoming both financial obstacles is only possible with support from her husband, so I understood why my mother emphasized that it was my father's suggestion that she learn how to drive. We both knew that not every woman of my mother's era and ilk would have been encouraged by their husband to learn how to drive. It is not lost on me that in one generation from my mother's, in the same country, Nigeria, I had the ability to decide when and how I was going to learn how to drive and paid for it without support from anybody, spouse or otherwise.

As we discussed how it felt for her to be able to drive and what this afforded her, I told my mother about how Saudi women had not been issued driver's licenses for fifty years before 2018. I also showed her a write-up for a 2018 exhibition organized by The Frick Pittsburgh's Car and Carriage Museum titled 'Driving the Disenfranchised—The Automobile's Role in Women's Suffrage', in which the museum writer stated "the automobile's central role provided a mechanism for women's identity— a means to free themselves from social and geographical limitations and to transcend prevailing gender stereotypes about their inherent mechanical naiveté and ineptitude. Female drivers challenged the notion that women ought to remain sequestered in the home. By the 1920s automobiles were a dominant cultural emblem of women's modernity, independence, and mobility."

Our conversation then delved into what it meant then and now for women to have and own the ability to drive. We compared her time, my era, and my daughter's time of today in different parts of the world and agreed on what the advocates for the 'Women to drive movement' in Saudi Arabia, say, "a woman driving is a declaration of her independence".

The Blue Datsun Pickup

After my mother got her driver's license, she drove my father's white *Renault 12* sedan to run errands while he used his assigned driver and army Land Rover to move around during the work week. On the weekends, they shared the Renault. According to my mother, the arrangement worked for them. My mother had stopped going to Kainji after she got her driver's license and had gone back to being a wholesaler of beers and soft drinks. She purchased the soft drinks from the Coca-Cola factory in Ibadan and the beers from the Nigerian Brewery factory also in Ibadan. Transporting her inventory was problematic as she had to hire trucks and vans every time she bought inventory, which ate into her profit margin.

My mother had no idea that my father was observing the transporting difficulties she was dealing with. According to her, out of the blue one day, he asked her what they could do to alleviate these problems and she responded that she was saving to buy a *Datsun* pickup. According to Wikipedia, "the Datsun Truck' as it was called "is a compact pickup truck made by Nissan in Japan from 1955 through 1997. It was originally sold under the Datsun brand, but this was switched to Nissan in 1983". My mother had seen the *Datsun 620* model that was first released in February 1972, at a car dealership in Ibadan in 1977 and it was the slightly new redesigned version made for 1978 car year, with changes to the grille and front bumper that she had seen. She also had her eye on the four-door crew cab variant that was offered in the Nigerian market. She assessed that she would be able to transport her children to school or on any outings and transport her inventory on her own when she took delivery at the factories. Her plan was to account for it as a business expense.

Me: "So, that is how you bought your blue Datsun Pickup?"

She smiled at my assumption with a twinkle in her eye.

My Mother: "Not at all."

Me: "What do you mean?"

My Mother: "Kunle had taken me a couple of times to the dealership, so he knew where it was. Your father, without me knowing asked Kunle about the dealership, and they went there, and he bought the Datsun Pickup in the royal blue color that I liked."

Me: "Wait, daddy bought it and you were unaware?" I asked, surprised.

My Mother: "Your father bought it, and he drove it to the house with Kunle behind him driving the Land Rover. I was in the dining room with one of you children checking your homework when your father walked in. He was in his army uniform. He called me to come outside and as I stepped outside on the steps of our Ibadan house to go to the open garage where we and the other tenants parked our cars, he gave me the keys to the pickup and told me that he had bought it for me as a gift. He said and I quote:" "You have supported the family financially since we have been married and that has given me room to breathe and not worry so much about our finances."

Me: "Wow! Oh my God, I did not know that. What did you say?"

My Mother: "I was speechless. I danced in the backyard, and

he joined me in the dancing, and we danced to where he had parked the car. The pickup was shining in the sunlight, brand sparkling new! It was a great day."

Me: "I don't remember this."

My Mother: "You were in boarding school. I think this was in 1978 and you were in your second year (Form 2) in secondary school."

This goes back to what I said in the introduction; finding out things about my mother that I did not know. This time though, it is my father whom I am learning things about. I had no idea he was a *romantic*! He pulled off a surprise for her with an enormous gift of something she wanted. That in my book, would beat any romantic gift a husband in our country with his limited finances could give at that time. In fact, I say with confidence, he would have beat many husbands in these contemporary times in pulling off giving his spouse such a large, unexpected gift. He knew she could save for it and buy it eventually, but he *stepped up* and decided to gift her to show his appreciation for sharing the financial burden of our family. Wow, good for him!

Chapter Ten

Friendship- First Time Making a True Friend: 1979

My mother was having a tough time after her beloved brother Awiki passed away in September 1978. So, making her first true friend in 1979 helped her a lot. Nigeria had returned to civilian rule in October 1979 after thirteen and a half years of military rule. You are probably shocked and asking how she had not made another true friend after her mother from when she was a young child to 1979 when she was forty-one years old. The operative word here is *'true'*. As she tells it, she had classmates in school that she had no chance to be close to as life as a pupil at the Native Administration Primary School, Ojobo, was not about playing after school. They all went their way when school was over to do chores for their mothers and fathers or go to the forest in some cases or accompany their mothers to the market to sell petty wares when it was market day at Ojobo or in another neighboring village.

After she got married in Lagos in 1956, all her friendships arose out of circumstances of being around fellow Izon people, or relatives of my father or their husbands were friends with my father. She enjoyed their company, but between trading and working to augment her family's income and raising her children, she was not afforded any time to foster true friendships.

∞∞∞

Mrs. Janet Adeagbo, a Cameroonian, lived on our street in

Ibadan. My mother met her while looking for a math lesson teacher for her two youngest children. She had heard through the neighborhood grapevine that a teacher of East Indian origin, who taught at the St. Patrick Grammar School, the secondary school in our 'Orita Bashorun' neighborhood, was giving math lessons to supplement his income at £4 per child a month. My mother contacted him and after a short discussion, they agreed that he would tutor her two youngest. Before hiring Mr. Kapoor, my mother was tutoring us with any problematic math issues we had. She set study time from 4 to 6 pm daily, and she would teach my siblings as I was in boarding school after she returned from supplying and selling drinks. After Mr. Kapoor started to tutor my siblings, she met Mrs. Adeagbo when she went to pick them up one evening.

Me: "How did you become friends with her?"

My Mother: "Mr. Kapoor had suggested that since it was just my two kids in that time slot, he would come to our house to teach them and save me the time of rushing back to pick them up. Mrs. Adeagbo was there when we were talking as her son's time slot was just before ours. She then asked if her son Kunle could join the math lessons at our house".

Me: "And you became friends then?"

My Mother: "We did. She was my first true friend that I met and made on my own and was not connected to being Izon or my husband. Every time she would bring Kunle who was your age for tutoring, we would chat and go to the lounge of their family hotel and continue talking. If you remember, their hotel was just a few feet from where we lived."

Me: "I remember."

Me: "How did your friendship grow?"

My Mother: "When my and her children were at school, she would come over in her black Datsun 280z sports car."

Me: "I forgot that you both drove Datsun cars."

My Mother: "We did. We would go to the market together. Sometimes she would accompany me in my pickup to the factories to buy drinks and we would converse about everything.

She told me about her life growing up in Cameroon and I told her about how I grew up at Ojobo."

Me: "Was that the first time, you talked about how you grew up with somebody?"

My Mother: "Yes, I believe so. We advised each other regarding our businesses and life generally."

Mrs. Adeagbo and my mother became best friends for all the years she lived in Ibadan till we moved away in 1982.

Chapter Eleven

A Curveball or a Pivot- Open to Interpretation: 1981-1982

Why do we say the things we do? I have always wondered. In North America, people use the expression, "life throws you curveballs". If you do not know or understand baseball (I only know that someone pitches and someone hits. I like Derek Jeter, but what exactly does a *shortstop* do? As far as I know, a shortstop is the baseball fielding position between second and third base, but that is all I know), this expression would seem strange to you, maybe even incomprehensible. A curveball in baseball according to the dictionary is "where it is a pitch thrown with a strong downward spin, causing the ball to drop suddenly and veer to the side as it approaches home plate". Used figuratively in the expression life throws you curveballs, it means "something which is unexpected, surprising, or disruptive". On the other hand, the word *pivot* which the Merriam-Webster dictionary defines as the following: "a shaft or pin on which something turns"; "a person, thing, or factor having a major or central role, function, or effect"; "a key player or position specifically: an offensive position of a basketball player standing usually with back to the basket to relay passes, shoot, or provide a screen for teammates"; and "a usually marked change", is now being used more in its last meaning listed here "a usually marked change". It has also evolved into being part of a verbal phrase the *act of pivoting.* The years that followed in Ibadan for my mother as she lived and raised her children and what she encountered at the end of her stay in Ibadan could fall between the category of a curveball or a pivot. It is open to interpretation.

As expected, the army transferred my father across our country Nigeria, with various stints back to Lagos where his army career began. My mother as they had agreed, held the fort in Ibadan and it was the family base. Her small business of trading beers and soft drinks was not as profitable as it was in Port Harcourt years before, because she was not getting the drinks at a controlled price. The price in Ibadan was subject to the economic laws of supply and demand, so her profit margin was small, and she was again constantly worried about money.

Me: "So what did you do?"

My Mother: "I was always looking for ways to expand my business, but there was nothing I could find at that time that would not take me out of the house for long periods of time and if you remember, some of you were still in primary school. Then a miracle in the form of Ajimmy, your father's nephew happened."

My uncle Ajimmy was the son of my father's oldest half-sister. My father and his oldest half-sister shared the same father but were born to different mothers. Ajimmy was very close to my parents as my father partially supported him in the early years of his marriage to my mother when Ajimmy was a university student.

Me: "How was Uncle Ajimmy a miracle? I remember we went to visit him one long holiday so he would help us understand secondary school math better."

My Mother: "This was after that. Ajimmy made things better for us. He sent me a telegram to come and see him and his family in Port-Harcourt. So, I went. With civilian rule, Ajimmy had just been appointed as the general manager of the Port-Harcourt Flour Mill in Port-Harcourt by the then governor of Rivers State, Melford Okilo. When I got to Port-Harcourt, Ajimmy asked me to take an instant passport picture and bring it to his office the next day. I took it to him, and he made me a flour distributor. He started me with one hundred bags of flour as I did not have the capital to support taking more than one hundred bags. The business model was to take the flour at the mill and immediately sell it to wholesale buyers at the mill gate. It felt like a miracle to see immediate profits. This is how I started the flour distributorship business and used it to feed our family and pay fees for years."

*My father and his nephew Ajimmy at
Ajimmy's graduation, circa 1969*

Planning For Every Eventuality

My mother, ever the business planner, had the inkling that the flour distribution business would not last long because the profit margin was too good to be true. Ajimmy's appointment as the general manager (GM) of Port Harcourt Flour Mill was also a political appointment that meant he could be removed at any time. My mother worried about this constantly. She discussed her worries with Ajimmy, and he suggested that if she opened a bakery, she would be entitled to getting flour from the Flour Mill even if he was no longer in his post as GM because she would be a manufacturer of flour end products like bread. The Port Harcourt Flour Mill regulations stated that manufacturers of flour end products must be given preference and should receive flour allocations. So, a new business idea of opening a bakery was born. Instead of jumping headfirst into it, my mother continued the flour distribution business for a while and started to observe and gather all the necessary information of what it would entail to open a bakery.

Developing The Business Plan For A Bakery

My mother flew back to Ibadan from Port Harcourt after she met Ajimmy to discuss her worries taking with her the possibility of the idea of opening a bakery. It was not something she had ever considered, but she liked the idea. As she sat in the plane, she said she considered the best possibility might be to open the bakery in her hometown of Ojobo with her sister Susannah. She did not think about talking to my father about it as they had always separated his work from her businesses, although all monies they earned and made respectively went into taking care of the family.

Me: "Did you do a recce as soon as you got back to Ibadan?"

My Mother: "After I got back to Ibadan from Port Harcourt, I travelled home to Ojobo a few weeks later to speak to my sister. I had made up my mind that I would open the bakery at Ojobo. It was not far from Port Harcourt, so the cost of transporting the flour to Ojobo would not be high and we would keep our costs low."

Me: "What did she say?"

My Mother: "Susannah was neither interested nor

convinced about the idea."

Me: "So what happened next?"

My Mother: "I went back to Ajimmy to tell him that my sister refused to entertain the idea or be part of it. Then, he convinced me to discuss the idea with his uncle, your father."

Me: "Did you discuss it with Daddy?"

My Mother: "I was not sure what he would think of it. At that time, I thought he was happy in his army career as he had not said anything about putting in his papers for retirement."

Me: "How did he take it when you told him the idea?"

My Mother: "When I raised the idea with him after talking to Ajimmy, he was sad and disappointed that I had not considered doing this with him first."

Me: "Was he angry?"

My Mother: "No, he was not. He trusted my judgment and asked me to tell him all the research that I had done. So, we discussed further and agreed that we would establish it in his hometown of Ndoro, because we had more land there and I would run it by myself to start with. We also agreed he would remain in the army and would come to see me at Ndoro as much as his career in the army allowed him to."

Me: "What happened next?"

My Mother: "Your father went back to Lagos after we discussed as he had come home to Ibadan for the weekend as he usually did. When he got back to Lagos, he talked to a friend of his in Lagos, who was French about our plans to open a bakery as that friend of his had experience running a bakery in Lagos. His friend suggested to him that it would be better if we did the bakery in a big way."

Me: "Big way?"

My Mother: "Yes. Your father returned to Ibadan the following weekend and told me about his friend's suggestion that we should go big."

Me: "So the plan changed to go big or go home?"

My mother looked at me clueless about what I meant.

Me: "Forget it." I said, realizing that my everyday parlance was gibberish to my mother.

My Mother: "We redrew our business plan getting rid of the idea of buying a mud oven."

Me: "What else did you change from your first business plan?"

My Mother: "We decided that we were going to purchase modernized baking machinery and since we did not have the capital for that, we agreed that we will take a bank loan as your father's friend had suggested."

Me: "I remember. The loan was for forty-five thousand Naira (₦45,000)."

For reference, ₦45,000 was worth $29,115 US Dollars at that time.

My Mother: "Yes it was. We approached a bank in Benin City and got a loan. Your father's good friends Papa Nayoka (Mr. Beke) and Seaman Ebitonmor were our sureties for the loan."

Me: "That was kind of them to act as your sureties. What happened after you got the loan?"

My Mother: "It was kind of them. After we got the loan, we ordered a mechanized oven, a loaf divider, and a mixer from France. Your father's French friend in Lagos helped us as he bought his bakery machines from the same company. We also ordered two bread milling machines locally from Benin City."

Me: "So things with the bakery kicked off?"

My Mother: "Yes, they did. We started to build our house and the bakery at Ndoro with our capital since we had taken the loan to buy the equipment we needed. And that sealed things for your father. Since we were building and would operate the bakery in a big way, we both knew I could not run it on my own, so he decided it was time to put in his retirement papers."

Me: "Wow! You were both so brave."

My Mother: "We went all in, but we were still afraid."

Shortly after my parents took the business loan, they hired a lawyer to register their holding company as *Alapbet Industries* and the bakery as *Lady Willy Enterprises*. Lady, as a play on my mother's name Lydia and she is a lady, and Willy for my father as his English first name was William.

Departure From Ibadan

After seven years in Ibadan, in August of 1982, my mother said goodbye to her best friend Mrs. Adeagbo, her acquaintances, and her neighbors to return to the Boloutoru creek that she had been so eager to leave twenty-six years prior.

Me: "You were going to Ndoro, a village similar and not far from Ojobo back to the creek to live. Earlier, you talked about the fear of a life of looking at the opposite riverbank day after day when you were younger and how you hoped to escape it. Now you were going back willingly to live there?"

My Mother: "It was not the same anymore. I was going back home voluntarily after twenty-six years to run our own business. I had traveled around Nigeria, lived amongst many tribes, raised my children, done business, and experienced a lot."

Two army-assigned lorries in the Nigerian Army colors were assigned to our family to get our possessions to Warri where they were loaded onto cargo boats. My mother packed the house within weeks and loaded the first lorry with plants and flowers that she would plant around the house at Ndoro, and she loaded the second lorry with all our earthly possessions, and off to a new life, it was.

Chapter Twelve

Back to her Roots- End of 1982 onwards

At the onset of their new business endeavor of opening the Lady Willy Bakery at Ndoro, my mother was overshadowed by the anxiety of whether the bakery would succeed.

Me: "What was your biggest concern?"

My Mother: "When we started, there was no market."

Me: "No market?"

My Mother: "Our prospective customers did not know about us, and I worried. We had two competitors in two villages: Torugbene and Tamigbe and they were not far from Ndoro and controlled all the market share. So, to attract customers, I would take the bread we had baked, load them into a canoe with Yamaha 5 horsepower engine and go hawk our bread in different villages down our Boloutoru Creek to advertise it. I went to my hometown Ojobo, Peretoru, and Agoro, a village at the mouth of the Atlantic Ocean."

Me: "Did this marketing effort work?"

My Mother: "It did. When the customers tasted the bread, they liked it. By the following week, they paddled their canoes from their villages to buy bread from our new bakery."

Me: "That must have been a relief."

My Mother: "It really was. We had exhausted our savings to start the bakery. The army was already processing your father's retirement papers, so the bakery had to work. There was no reversing your father's decision to retire."

Me: "I had no idea that you were so stressed at that time."

My Mother: "It was stressful. You were in Lower Six in

Federal Government Girls College, Benin, I believe. We used your father's salary that was still coming in to pay school fees for you all."

Me: "I was in Lower Six. Things must have been tight."

My Mother: "Things were very tight, but things got better when the business started growing and customers were purchasing our bread. Your father was stationed in Benin City in his last posting when his retirement papers were being processed and I visited him only a couple of times there."

Me: "Then his retirement was processed afterward?"

My Mother: "Yes, it was by the end of 1983. It was a good thing as running the bakery, going to Port Harcourt to get the flour from the Flour Mill, and going to Warri every other week to get materials like sugar, vegetable oil, and other raw materials, was getting too much for me. We needed him at Ndoro to join me in managing the business."

Me: "How did things progress with the bakery after he was officially retired from the army?"

My Mother: "We shared the burden of running the bakery equally. The business grew and sometimes we both had to travel to Port Harcourt, starting the journey from Ndoro by boat to Bomadi and then by car to Port Harcourt to go buy flour. He would go with one truck, and I would go with the another after we had bought our flour allocation. Then we would supervise the loading of the flour into boats at Warri waterside on the return journey."

The business was good for the first few years, my mother relates. It was so good that my father did not pursue putting in his gratuity and pension applications to the army for the first few years. She urged him to get the ball rolling, so they would have a rainy-day fund for emergencies, and he did

∞ ∞ ∞

Ebb & Flow

By the late eighties into the early nineties, like all marriages and businesses, my mother says she and my father had gone through a natural series of ebbs and flows during the years after they moved to Ndoro and were running their bakery together. She says there was friction between them from time to time, and many a time she was "furious about certain events as it concerned the management of the bakery." Their management styles according to her were different, so gradually, they came to a decision that she would diversify some of her energy to other businesses but continue to oversee how some things were managed in the bakery to ensure monies from the bakery would be used to educate us children and take care of our needs.

∞∞∞

Becoming And Unbecoming An Empty Nester

By the late nineteen eighties, my mother was becoming an empty nester. Her life entailed ensuring her children's secondary and post-secondary tuition fees and our other needs were taken care of and she was just ten minutes from Ojobo by speedboat which enabled her to regularly go visit her mother to make sure she was doing well. As she navigated the transition of not having any of us children living permanently at home in Ndoro, her older cousin/ uncle Elakemfa passed away and she traveled to Bomadi for his burial. When she was at Bomadi for the burial, she learned about the death of her maternal cousin from her grandmother's side of the family in Cameroon. Her cousin had lived in Cameroon since he had gone there to trade in the late sixties, so his corpse was to be brought back to Bomadi for burial.

To give some background on my maternal great-grandmother Ebitoubo's side of the family and how my mother kept the connection to her relatives on that side of her family and why both the deaths of Elakemfa and her other cousin changed my mother's life and her plans, my great-grandmother, Ebitoubo had four sisters and they had all married men in different villages along the Boloutoru creek. The way our Izon culture works is if anything happened to any of them or their descendants in those villages, the others would all congregate there to support them. From Ebitoubo's descendants, my mother was the only one financially capable of participating when something happened in their extended family at the time. If there was a wedding, death, or if anything of import happened, she would go to Bomadi, Ebitoubo's hometown to represent her grandmother side of the family and make the necessary contribution of whatever is asked of all family members. That meant Elakemfa's death as the oldest male in her grandmother's extended family was significant. He had been responsible for many of their extended family obligations and one of those obligations was regarding one of my mother's grandaunts. She had left the husband she had married many years ago in the village of Isampou in the Boloutoru creek, to marry someone else without my great-grandmother's family repaying the bride price and the dowry to the previous husband. My mother's grandaunt passed away a few years after she married her second husband and she had borne many children with him. My mother was still a young girl when this all happened but consequently, per Izon tradition, all her grandaunt's children that she had given birth to after leaving that first husband and their offspring were considered 'slaves' of the family of the first husband. Elakemfa had been negotiating the payment of the monies owed when he passed. Coincidentally, my mother's grandaunt's first husband also passed at the same time, meaning if the monies were not repaid, her children would be deemed part of his estate- 'slaves' to be shared among his relatives. To prevent this, my mother and her maternal extended family quickly repaid the monies which are termed 'Komolojo' in Izon. I still cannot believe this is a thing in the Izon culture. Repayment of bride price, refund of dowry, human beings being deemed *slaves* like chattel of an estate? As strange as this all sounds, it is still the Izon tradition and culture that Izon women are still subject to.

Coming back to my mother's cousin who died in Cameroon around the same time Elakemfa died, his corpse was accompanied to Bomadi by all the wives he had taken in Cameroon, and the children whom he had borne with them. My mother and her maternal relatives were in a quandary about what to do to help the family he left behind, especially the young children. His only sister of the same parents already had five children of her own and had no means to care for her nieces and nephews that her brother had left behind. My mother and her relatives had back-and-forth discussions, and in the end, my mother volunteered to take one of the children as her own. He was just seven years old and became my brother, Alex. Though she did not consult my father before making her decision, she says he was okay with it, and years later, when my brother Alex as a young adult, asked my father if he could change his last name to ours, my father supported it and gave him permission to do so.

Chapter Thirteen

The Onset of Hypertension and Other Health Issues: 1979-present

As you know, one of the things you get asked when you go to a doctor is your family health history. Knowing it according to the United States Center for Disease Control (CDC) is not enough, you must act on it. All families share genes and asking my mother to share her life story with me, has given me the opportunity to have a record of the diseases and health conditions in our family as best as I can. The CDC in its *Family Health History: The Basics* posted on its website, states that "most people have a family health history of at least one chronic disease, such as cancer, heart disease, and diabetes. If you have a close family member with a chronic disease, you may be more likely to develop that disease yourself, especially if more than one close relative has (or had) the disease or a family member got the disease at a younger age than usual." This is scary, but I am sure you agree that it is essential to our health to have this information.

My mother started to suffer from hypertension during her years at Ibadan because of stress and certain issues regarding her children. As hypertension typically develops over the course of several years, and usually medical experts say a person does not notice any symptoms, my mother did not know that she was beginning to enter the high blood pressure spectrum until she was smack dab in the middle of it. The onset of her hypertension was no different and could be a poster example in any anatomy textbook.

Me: "When did you first have hypertension symptoms?

My Mother: "I did not know I had the symptoms, but I was stressed out about many things, and I felt like my life had ended at certain times in Ibadan because I had no idea what to do. One day in 1979, I believe the stress got too much and I fainted. I was rushed to the ER in Ibadan, and upon getting there, they checked my blood pressure and found it so high that they diagnosed that I was close to having a stroke. That was when my hypertension started, and I have had it ever since."

For reference, high blood pressure can cause damage to your blood vessels and organs, especially the brain, heart, eyes, and kidneys.

Me: "Then it got worse when you were living at Ndoro?"

My Mother: "Yes. I was on blood pressure medication from 1979 in Ibadan, but I collapsed again years later in Ndoro and only Alex and your cousin Bose were with me when this happened. I was rushed to the clinic at Ojobo, and when your father arrived back to Ndoro from Port Harcourt where he had gone to buy flour, he took me to the Eku Baptist Hospital near Sapele."

My mother's hypertension got worse, and, in the spring of 2001, the summer of 2002, and the fall of 2004, she traveled to Germany where one of my sisters and I lived for a medical checkup that covered a checkup of her heart and other parts of her body. The cardiologist in Rotenburg (Wuemme) in Germany who examined her on her first visit put her on beta blockers for five years to cause her heart to beat more slowly and with less force to lower her blood pressure. The general practitioner who also examined her and referred her to the cardiologist put her on customized blood pressure medication suited for her body that she takes to this day.

Fuchs' Dystrophy

Over the years, my mother's vision deteriorated in her left eye, and she got glasses to correct her vision with no success. While she was in Germany the first time to get her heart checked and to bring her high blood pressure under control, her GP recommended she see an eye specialist. She saw an ophthalmologist and he diagnosed that she had *Fuchs' dystrophy*.

Per John Hopkins Medicine, "Fuchs' dystrophy is a genetic disease affecting the cornea. Although a patient is born with the condition, it is not detectable or symptomatic until middle age or later. During the disease's progression, the layer of cells (endothelium) responsible for maintaining proper fluid levels in the cornea will deteriorate and cause tiny bumps (guttae) to form on the back of the cornea. When enough cells are lost, fluid builds up in the cornea, resulting in swelling. This swelling, called corneal edema, causes clouding or blurring of vision."

The Mayo Clinic states in addition that "the genetic basis of the disease is complex — family members can be affected to varying degrees or not at all."

The German ophthalmologist did not sugarcoat the diagnosis to my mother. He informed her that the disease was in an advanced stage and at that time the damage was irreversible. He advised that she should take care of her right eye in which she still had relatively good vision and should continue to monitor therapies that could offer a treatment for her damaged eye. Today ophthalmologists are doing corneal transplant surgeries and Endothelial keratoplasty, a particular form of corneal transplant surgery to treat Fuchs' dystrophy.

A gut punch about Fuchs' dystrophy is that one of the risk factors is Fuchs' dystrophy is more common in women than in men.

This is my mother's story, but here I will share something with you here about me that connects to my mother suffering from Fuchs' dystrophy to buttress that knowing your family health history could be vital to your health. In 2006, I started noticing an impairment of the vision in my left eye, and I made an appointment and went to see the same ophthalmologist that had seen my mother five years before in Rotenburg-Wuemme, Germany. He examined my eye and he diagnosed me with the same disease of Fuchs' dystrophy. Fortunately, in 2009 in Canada, I had a corneal transplant surgery to treat the disease. Knowing your family health history is vital as the CDC and other health organizations around the world recommend. Because I knew my mother's disease, I was able to highlight it to the doctor when I noticed I had similar symptoms.

My mother, visiting in Rotenburg (Wuemme) Germany, in 2001

Chapter Fourteen

O Grave, where is thy Victory: 2001-2019

My mother is the last living person from the "*nuclear family*" she grew up in. I am not using the term "*nuclear family*" here in the way it is used today, which is figurative. The Merriam-Webster dictionary website states that the term nuclear family "comes from an extension of those varied scientific applications of the word *nucleus*. In addition to astronomy, botany, and other technical applications, the word nucleus has also since the mid-18th century meant simply *a basic or essential part*, with many examples of the term describing people considered core to some organization or effort". The Oxford English Dictionary cites Bronislaw Malinowski, a Polish-British Anthropologist, considered a founder of social anthropology, as the coiner of the term. The Merriam-Webster dictionary website on *The History of Nuclear Family* in my opinion to be humorous, states that "in coining nuclear family, Malinowski was hitching a sensible descriptor to the word family to create what is now one of the world's basic familial designators. No one could have known at the time that that descriptor would go *nuclear*."

I am using the term going back to the senses of its parent word *nucleus* meaning *kernel* or more simply *something essential*. My mother's kernel of people growing up and as a young girl on the cusp of womanhood was her mother, her sister, and later her husband, whom she married when she was just shy of her eighteenth birthday. They all passed away between 2001 to 2019, leaving her to carry on living with the memories of the lives she shared with them.

I am in awe of my mother's strength as we talk about the loss of the three people who knew her best as a child and a young woman. As I watch her through the screen of my iPhone, I try to find words to say to her to give her some solace, but I cannot find any that would suffice. I recite in my head continuously the second question Apostle Paul asked in his first letter to the Corinthians in certain versions of the Bible (chapter fifteen, verse fifty-five) - "o grave, where is thy victory" to find comforting words. Many theologians say this verse is "the cry of triumph over death that Paul thinks Christians will make when the time comes that death can no longer steal their mothers, fathers, sisters, brothers, daughters, and sons." I have no idea if this is true, but I hope for all of us that a time would come when we would no longer feel the sting of death and there would be no need for graves.

2001- Granny Okpe's Death

Susan Wiggs, an American author stated that "there is something about losing a mother that is permanent and indefinable— a wound that never quite heals." I am fortunate to still have my mother, but my mother has lost her mother and she is no exception to how the loss of her mother still affects her after twenty-one years.

My granny Okpe suffered from a stroke in late 2000 whilst my mother was visiting her cousin at Ojobo from Ndoro. On the day it happened, my mother narrates that someone rushed into her cousin's house to tell her something was wrong with her mother.

Me: "What did you do after the person rushed in with the news?"

My Mother: "I ran as fast as I could to my mother's house and saw that she had suffered a stroke."

Me: "Did you get someone from the hospital at Ojobo to confirm what you thought had happened?"

My Mother: "At that time, the Government Hospital at Ojobo

was equipped with a doctor and some nurses, so we sent for someone to come and see my mother."

Me: "And they confirmed the diagnosis that she had suffered a stroke?"

My Mother: "They did and said there was nothing they could do. My mother never spoke again after she suffered the stroke."

Me: "So what did you do?"

My Mother: "She was in a vegetative state, but I hired someone to care for her."

Me: "Was there any change to her condition?"

My Mother: "There was no improvement, but I always visited her, sat with her, and talked to her."

Me: "I don't remember anymore how long granny was in that state."

My Mother: "She was in that state for about six months. I was at Ojobo when she passed away."

Me: "I can't imagine how tough that was for you."

My Mother: "It was tough, but we expected it. I was with her as I knew she was dying. In her last days, she did not eat or drink. Susannah and I held her till she took her last breath. She died in her room where she had given birth to us and lived all her married life and life as a widow after my father died."

My granny Okpe's burial was not held immediately after she died as there was an election taking place at the time, so it was dangerous because people were getting killed. As Izon tradition dictates, my granny's marital compound people i.e., my mother's paternal relatives determined that her corpse should be taken to the mortuary in Bomadi as Ojobo did not have one. They also set the dates for her wake-keeping and burial. Because the dates were set far ahead, my mother arranged for her mother's corpse to be taken to the mortuary at Bomadi. On November 14, 2001, granny Okpe's wake-keeping was held at Ojobo, and she was buried the next day, November 15, in her hometown of Peretoru as is the Izon custom.

Me: "Do you often think of granny so long after her death?"

My Mother: "I think of her often and I miss her still. Now that I am living in Ojobo where I grew up with her in her house not far from where mine is located, I think of her all the time and the conversations we had when I was growing up. I also think of those last months when she was sick. Though her death was expected at the end, it was still painful."

Me: "I am sorry."

My Mother: "Thank you."

2019-Aunty Susannah's Death

On the website healgrief.org, it is stated that "the death of a sibling is the most neglected loss in adult life". It is further opined on the site that "the loss of a sibling means the loss of someone who knew your formative past, which might trigger feelings of guilt over unsolved sibling issues or a sense of abandonment". So, I ask you, how much worse would it be if you are the adult sibling left behind when your sibling dies by suicide? That is what happened to my mother and apparently, no one tells you what to do in those circumstances.

As you know from earlier in my mother's story, she was twelve years old in 1950 when her sister was born. Because of the age gap between them, my mother saw her sister Susannah more like a daughter to her than a younger sister. She took care of her sister when her mother would go to the forest until she left Ojobo for Lagos to get married. My mother tells me that when her sister was a teenager, she came to live with her whenever she wanted and when my aunt became a young mother, my mother took care of her niece, so her sister could still pursue her education or anything else she wanted to do. Even when they were both adults, my mother always planned her life with her sister in mind.

So, when my mother started noticing something was off with her sister six years before her death, she was bothered. Their normal close sister-relationship was eroding, and she could not get a handle on what was going on with her sister.

Me: "What exactly did you notice?"

My Mother: "I could not reach her whenever I called her."

Me: "When did this start?"

My Mother: "This was in 2013. I remember exactly. You people had sent me money and from that money, I sent my sister N30,000 Naira. Initially, my sister called me to thank me but after a few days, she sent the money back to me with someone who was coming to Ndoro from Ojobo."

Me: "I remember you telling me about that. Did she say why she sent it back?"

My Mother: "She did not and I wondered what was happening, so I went to Ojobo to see her at her husband's house."

Me: "Did you see her?"

My Mother: "No, I was not able to see her, and every time whenever I would go to Ojobo from Ndoro for any events and try to see her, I was never able to reach her or see her. People at Ojobo kept telling her that my sister looked unwell and was getting very thin."

Me: "Did you send messages to her children?"

My Mother: "I did, but they did not respond to my messages until I saw my niece, her oldest at Ojobo when I went for a burial. I asked what was happening with my sister and she could not give me any answers. We talked about what could be going on, but my niece said she did not understand either but felt that many things were going on with her mother."

Me: "Then what happened?"

My Mother: "Around May of 2019, my sister called me from the blue, and told me that she would like to see me. I had not heard from her in six years.

Me: "Were you shocked when you got her call and heard her voice?'

My Mother: "I was shocked, but I was also very happy to hear from her."

Me: "What did she say?"

My Mother: "Her exact words were: "I would like to come to see you as anyone can die at any time"."

Me: "She said that?" I asked, shocked. I knew they conversed, but I did not my aunt's exact words.

My Mother: "Yes she did."

So, my mother invited her sister to come to Ndoro to see her and suggested that they spend some days together when she came. My aunty Susannah acquiesced to my mother's suggestion, but she never made the trip to Ndoro as they agreed.

Three months later, my aunty Susannah took her own life.

My mother got the news from her two oldest children, my siblings, who had received the news from my oldest living maternal uncle. It was an extremely difficult death notification that also involved my paternal cousins who lived in Ndoro.

Me: "May I ask how you felt when you got the news of aunty Susannah's death?"

My Mother: "I was and am still heartbroken knowing she must have suffered a lot and been in a lot of pain for her to commit suicide. Our culture frowns on suicide and she knew this, so she must have felt she had no choice."

Me: "Do you ever think, maybe we could have pushed her children and done more to demand to know what was going on with her?"

My Mother: "I believe I tried my best for her throughout her life, so I do not feel I could have done more. We could not have forced her children or her husband to tell us what was going on. But seeing her grave every day in front of my house now in my compound is hard and makes me always wonder what must have happened to her those six years that I could not reach her."

2005-Alex's Death

You would think that my mother had suffered enough death in her life in the span of eighteen years, losing her mother, her husband, and her sister, but she also had to endure the death of the boy that became her son at a later stage of her life in a workplace accident.

Me: "How did you hear about Alex's death?"

My Mother: "Your father and I saw Alex often as he was working at the oil location not far from Ndoro. He would come to

Ndoro to visit us when he had days off."

Me: "I did not know that."

My Mother: "Yes, he did. We had heard about the explosion that happened, but we did not know he did not make it out, until someone came to inform us."

Me: "I still remember getting the news."

My Mother: "Since Alex's death, I find it difficult to go to Bomadi or pass it on my way anywhere because he is buried there."

Chapter Fifteen

17 Days in 2010

My mother was married to my father for fifty-four years, four months, and two days (54yrs. 4 mths. & 2 days); exactly six hundred and fifty months (652 mths.); and nineteen thousand, eight hundred and forty-five days (19,845 days), before she became his widow. With the nature of my father's job in the Nigerian Army over the years of their marriage and after he retired from the army, my mother spent many days away from him due to travel, family events, visiting us their children in various places, etc., but in the end, she says she feels blessed to have spent the last 17 days of his life with him.

By 2010, my mother was spending more time at Ojobo trying to complete the house she was building, which in our Izon culture is necessary as a person's last place of rest is in their hometown and not where they married i.e., their husband's hometown. While she was doing that, my father was still running their bakery at Ndoro. That was the rhythm of their lives until late July 2010 when my mother went to Yenagoa for a one-week visit and has just returned to Ojobo.

Me: "So, you were in Yenagoa when Daddy fell sick?"

My Mother: "I had been in Yenagoa for a week and had just returned to Ojobo when your sister called me that she had received a call from one of your father's workers in Ndoro that your father was sick."

Me: "The sickness resulted from his motorcycle accident that happened a few months before?"

My Mother: "Yes. The injuries he sustained on his legs from

the accident had gotten infected so his worker who had called your sister brought him from Ndoro to the waterside at Bomadi and your sister picked him up from there and took him to the hospital in Yenagoa. She called me after she picked him up from Bomadi and I made my way to Yenagoa."

Me: "Then what happened?"

My Mother: "He was already admitted to the hospital (the Federal Medical Centre) when I got to Yenagoa if you remember?"

Me: "I remember."

My Mother: "He was in the hospital for 17 days before he passed away."

Me: "I have always wondered what you spoke about in those last days. Do you mind telling me?"

My Mother: "I don't mind. When they initially admitted him, he was aware of his surroundings."

Me: "Then things changed?"

My Mother: "Yes, they did. He started getting confused and began to hallucinate after a day or two in the hospital. I think the infection had spread in his bloodstream. Though he was slightly aware of his surroundings in those 17 days, he told me he was seeing his dead friends. He kept asking if I could see them as well. "

Me: "What did you tell him when he asked if you could see his dead friends?"

My Mother: "I told him that I could not see anyone. I spent every day with him in the hospital, but I was not allowed to spend the night. I would go to the hospital daily immediately after breakfast and stay until 6 pm. Then your younger brother would spend the night with him daily in the hospital."

Me: "Did he say anything specific to you after he began to get confused?"

My Mother: "The only coherent thing he said to me was that we should care for his worker who had been very helpful to him, the same one that informed your sister that he had fallen ill and took him to Bomadi waterside before your sister brought him to the hospital. He also noted that some of his customers from the small village of Agoro, owed him a lot of money."

Me: "Is that all he said?"

My Mother: "He also said that we had done a good job regarding our children, but we always acknowledged that to each other during that period."

Me: "That was nice."

My Mother: "It was, but I recall that those last 17 days felt like a part of me was gone as in all the fifty-four years we were married, he was never seriously sick. I knew he was not going to make it. Despite all the treatment the doctors were giving him, his condition did not improve."

Me: "What did you do? Did he know that he was dying?"

My Mother: "I tried to talk to him any time I was in the hospital room with him. I encouraged him to concentrate and believe the doctors would cure him. He always asked me whenever I said that if I thought the treatments would work."

Me: "On the day he died, you were not in the hospital. What happened?"

My Mother: "On the day he passed away, I was not allowed to see him. It was August 24, 2010. Thinking back, I suspect they knew he would not survive the day. Around 11 am that day, your sister, your paternal cousin, and your sister's husband came back to your sister's house where I was staying to see me. My heart skipped when I saw them as it was unusual for them to return to the house in the middle of the workday. Then, they told me your father had passed away."

Me: "How did you receive the news? I still vividly remember how I felt when I got the news."

My Mother: "Though it was expected, I did not have the strength to cry as I wanted to because I was so weak from all the worrying."

The Death Of One's Husband- Izon Rites

Unlike the death of a man's wife, when a woman loses her husband, Izon tradition dictates certain rites. My mother returned to Ndoro, my father's hometown as Izon tradition called for immediately after his passing to start the mandated period of mourning. She also had to be there to start getting things ready for his burial. One of my sisters had flown in from Germany two days after my father died and advised and organized for my mother to return to Ndoro.

Fortunately for my mother, she did not have to endure the psychosocial problems that sometimes befall widows because of traditional Izon burial rites. Some widows must sleep on hard cold floors in the name of 'proper traditional mourning rites', which leads to them catching fevers. They also sometimes endure disinheritance, suspicion, and other degrading inhuman treatment by their late husband's relatives which frustrates them, making many feel hopeless. We shielded my mother from anyone mistreating her and on October 31, 2010, at Ndoro, in front of the house my mother had built with my father, she was able to bury her husband and we were able to bury our father, two months and a week after he passed away.

My parents, in Port Harcourt, Nigeria, circa December 2000.

*Probably the last picture of my parents
together, in Yenagoa, Nigeria, circa 2005.*

Chapter Sixteen

Let's Play Twenty Questions: 2022

While writing this book, I discovered the card game- *Parents are Human* developed by Candace (a young Taiwanese-American) and Joseph (a young Chinese-American) with the goal that they say, "if it helped just one other person share a meaningful moment with their mom or dad, it would all be worth it". The game is a bilingual card game that on their website is described as "helps you spark deep conversations with your parents & loved ones". I am fortunate not to have needed a game like that to have deep conversations with my mother as she agreed to share her life story with me. I am also incredibly blessed that I get to tell it for me, for my children and her other descendants and for posterity. Nonetheless, after we went through her story chronologically for this book, I realized I was still missing some things about my mother because I was letting some of my memories from my vantage point skew some events from her perspective. So, to remove any tainting my memories was causing from the equation that makes up who my mother is, I am going to use the best game I know to get to know someone intimately- the classic game of *20 Questions*. Many people find it is the perfect way to get to know someone very well, so I am hoping I can use the format for my purposes here. But I am also cognizant that some of the typical questions might not be appropriate as it is a 'flirting game' and she is my mother, so I did some additional research on what questions would work and I came across an article titled *"24 Questions You Should Ask Your Parents, While You Can"*, by Amy Gibson, the former Managing Editor of Blogs, HuffPost Canada, originally published in April 2016 and updated on December 24, 2019.

The Twenty Questions I Asked My Mother And The Answers She Gave

Here are the twenty questions in no order that I asked my mother to further glean her perspective on the events and decisions that shaped her; some of the questions I came up with, others I borrowed from the classic game and the rest I took from Ms. Gibson's article. Then my mother's answers followed the questions.

1. Me: "What is your greatest wish now at this point in your life?'

My Mother: "My greatest wish after I had raised my children, was to complete my house to my taste and live there in my hometown, Ojobo for the rest of my days. Now you, your sister, and your brother after thirty-eight years after I laid the foundation of my house helped me to complete it beyond what I could have imagined. My great wish now is to live the rest of my days here at Ojobo in the comfort that the three of you are keeping me. I am happy. I talk to my children, my remaining siblings, and cousins by video conference whenever I want from the comfort of my home, so I have no cause for concern, and I am grateful for my life."

2. Me: "What is your favorite memory of your childhood?"

My Mother: "None that I can remember. I grew up in a polygamous family and our household was just my mother and me before my sister Susannah was born when I was twelve years old. I was born a girl child in a boy-preferred Izon world, so I grew up pitying my mother because she had no son. I had to learn to do what a son would do for his mother. This was tough and physical work."

3. Me: "What is your scariest memory from childhood?"

My Mother: "I have two scariest memories from my childhood. One was when my mother was pregnant with my sister. I was terrified my mother would die during pregnancy or childbirth, as many women did at that time. I was afraid that if my mother died, I would be all alone and an orphan as the mothers in our world cared for their children. The second one was waking up in my grandmother's fishing camp next to a boa constrictor one day. I woke up next to something that was cold and when I turned, it was a big boa constrictor. I jumped up and screamed for my grandmother."

4. Me: "What is your favorite food? I should know that."

My Mother: "Rice and tomato and pepper stew".

5. Me: "What would you have done differently in your life if you had my choices?"

My Mother: "I don't know if I would have done things differently. As you know, I did not have the choices you had. I made the best life for myself, my children, and my mother on what was afforded to me."

6. Me: "What do you think about now when you reflect on your life?"

My Mother: "I think about the fact that I am my father's oldest surviving daughter. I think about being the only one left from my childhood family; my husband, my mother, and my sister are all dead. And I think about living through my children."

7. Me: "What do you still wish for?"

My Mother: "I have always wanted to see more of the world. Because of you and your sister, I traveled abroad to Germany.

My dream was to see more of the world and explore more. Now though the spirit is willing, the body is weak."

8. Me: "What is your favorite place in the world?"
My Mother: "My house at Ojobo is my favorite place. I also really liked our house and the city when we were stationed in Port Harcourt."

9. Me: "What is your biggest regret?"
My Mother: "None really. I tend not to regret what I cannot go back and change."

10. Me: "How would your mother describe you?"
My Mother: "My mother saw me as a good daughter that did everything to take care of her."

11. Me: "What do you miss the most about the 'olden days'?"
My Mother: "Frankly, nothing."

12. Me: "What type of books did you like reading when you were younger?"
My Mother: "My favorite subject in school was math, so I liked reading books that had math problems."

13. Me: "What is your favorite type of TV show or movie?"
My Mother: "I watch movies now to pass time and not be bored. I do not like our Nigerian movies that showcase medicine men and *Juju*. I like movies that inspire, and I can learn something from them."

14. Me: "What is your favorite type of music or song?"

My Mother: "My favorite song is Jim Reeves *This World is Not My Home*. I am not interested in dancing, so I only like music that I can listen to. Your father was the dancer in our family."

15. Me: "If you could live your life all over again, would you change anything?"

My Mother: "I would get better educated so I would be capable of doing many things by myself and would have been able to rely more on myself."

16. Me: "What Izon tradition did you hate the most growing up that you wish was banned at that time?"

My Mother: "The female genital circumcision – mutilation. I wish it never existed. It was a horrible and painful experience."

17. Me: "What family tradition in our family did you cherish the most?"

My Mother: "Study time. I loved when we would all be around the dining table studying and all of you children talking about how the school day or school days had gone. "

18. Me: "When you were growing up, who did you look up to or who inspired you?"

My Mother: "My father was whom I looked up to growing up. He was an important man, and everyone respected him in Ojobo and other surrounding villages and towns. I wanted to be a person of substance like him."

19. Me: "What are some of your happiest memories?"

My Mother: "Apart from some great memories of and with you kids, my happiest memory was when your father bought me a car, the pickup without my knowing, and surprised me with the keys and the car documents in my name. I bring out that memory almost every day when I think about him. I think about how happy I was, his laughter, and how we both danced outside to see the car. I have never been so surprised and felt so appreciated."

20. Me: "What advice would you give your young self?"
My Mother: "I would advise her to always think well before making any decision."

Chapter Seventeen

So Far, For Now: Present Day

To find the best way to wrap up my mother's story without writing a conclusion that signifies an ending, which is not the case as mother lives and breathes and hopefully has more extraordinary chapters in her life by her own determination, I stumbled upon a 2007 list *"What to Look for When You Read a Biography"* prepared by Sasha Lauterbach and Marion Reynolds for the 'History Makers', a professional development program presented by the John F. Kennedy Presidential Library Education Department in partnership with Boston Public Schools, supported by a Teaching American History Grant from the U.S. Department of Education. They state among other things that a good biography presents the facts about a person's life; the author's viewpoint; the information included and left out; if what is written in the biography is true; can you check what evidence a biographer used; if you can check what evidence a biographer used, and they then ask you the reader, to remember that because something is in a book does not mean it is true and to think about why some people have many biographies written about them and others have few or none. I am glad and relieved I did not see this list before I started writing the story of my mother as it would have put me off daring to even think of telling her story. The criteria in the list above do not apply here. This is not a biography per se, it is the story of my mother so far, for now.

Hence, the best place to wrap things up will be to come back to the second question I asked at the beginning of the introduction- why you should care to read the story of my mother? After all, she is not your mother; you do not know her, and she is neither famous nor a historical figure. But I bet, you can relate to wanting to know from whom you come and whence you came. In over half a century on this earth, I have yet to meet anyone who does not want to know where they come from, or who their parents, or their grandparents or their great-grandparents, or other ancestors are. I believe that is one of the reasons (*I am not presumptuous to think it is the only reason*), why people pay $24 U.S. dollars to companies like *Ancestry.com* to have a membership on their site and create family trees on their accounts. Even cheaper versions like *FindMyPast* use the "Family Tree Builder" application and you need a paid subscription to view your records after your two-week free trial. Many elementary/ primary school curricula include the '*create your family tree*' assignment. Everyone has a need to trace their history and this need starts early in life.

My mother's story as you can imagine is uniquely hers and ours. I wrote it to her, for her, and for all her descendants, now and forever. The names of the people, the places and the languages in my mother's story might seem foreign to you, but her fears, her hopes, her dreams, and her goals, are as universal as lying under the sun or watching a full moon shine wherever you are on this planet of ours. We all had or have mothers and fathers and for that reason, I implore you to see them as persons in their own individuality and humanity and not just as your parents. Hopefully, you will learn what makes them who they are as I have learned more about what makes my mother who she is.

Three More Things

To borrow Oprah's phrase, what I now 'know for sure' about mother are three additional things: she is funny as heck without meaning to be (I knew that, but I can confirm it now); she says *"thank you" "thank you" "thank you"* three times in succession (I never noticed this before this exercise); and she has an elephant's memory and forgets nothing (I knew that, and it has not changed despite her advanced age).

Bibliography & Filmography

Johnson, Kirsten. (Director & Filmmaker) *Dick Johnson is Dead* Netflix, 2020

Cooper, Anderson. *All There Is with Anderson Cooper - Podcast Episode 05-Anticipatory Grief-* October. 2022

Coogler, Ryan. (Director) *Black Panther* (film) Marvel Studios and distributed by Walt Disney Studios Motion Pictures, 2018

Mbarga, Nico and his band Rocafil Jazz *Sweet Mother* Rogers All Stars, 1976

Tamuno, Tekena N. *Nigeria and Elective Representation 1923–1947* Heinemann, 1966

Olomojobi, Yinka. *Marriage in Nigeria Across Ages: Problems and Prospects* SSRN, 2016

Ceballo Rosaro. Graham, Erin., and Hart. Jamie. *Silent and Infertile: An Intersectional Analysis of the Experiences of Socioeconomically Diverse African American Women with Infertility* University of Michigan Study, 2015

Grose. Jessica. *Why Women Do the Household Worrying* New York Times Parenting Newsletter, 2021

Daminger, Allison. *The Cognitive Dimension of Household Labor* American Sociological Review, 2019

Clark Bekederemo, J.P. *Ibadan* Mbari, 1962

Miz Alb, "Chicago by Carl Sandburg", *Poem Analysis*, 17 June 2021, https://poemanalysis.com/carl-sandburg/chicago/.

The Frick Pittsburgh *Driving the Disenfranchised—The Automobile's Role in Women's Suffrage* 2018

Merriam-Webster dictionary website on *The History of Nuclear Family*

Gibson, Amy. *24 Questions You Should Ask Your Parents, While You*

Can HuffPost Canada, 2016, and updated in 2019
Lauterbach, Sasha., and Reynolds, Marion. *What to Look for When You Read a Biography* John F Kennedy Presidential Library Education Department, 2007

Acknowledgements

Writing is a solitary endeavour, but you still need people who support you and shepherd your efforts all the way especially when self-doubt creeps in. As this is my first foray into writing and finishing a book, I am grateful to my children, Jordan and Chelsea, and my ex-husband, Olaf who always believed I could do this and encouraged me to take a leap. I owe my sister, Theresa who is dogged in helping me track down photos of my mother and other members of our family that are part of my mother's story and let me know writing our mother's story "is a lovely and sweet thing to do." I am grateful to my brother Patrick, who always offered me words of encouragement, prayer and support. I want to particularly thank my daughter, Chelsea, who took many hours from her busy life to read my manuscript, offering feedback and advice, correcting my grammar and so much more. And most importantly, I am deeply indebted to my mother, Lydia, who agreed to share her very personal story with me and gave me permission to tell it.

About The Author

P. P. Atte

P.P. Atte was born in Lagos, Nigeria and grew up primarily in two of the biggest cities in Nigeria, Lagos and Ibadan. She studied law at the University of Benin in Benin City and attended the Nigerian Law School in Lagos, Nigeria. After practising law from 1989 to 1996 in Lagos, she left Nigeria to pursue postgraduate studies in Germany. In 2007, after eleven years in Germany, she immigrated to Calgary, Alberta, Canada, with her family. She is a practising lawyer and an entrepreneur in Calgary, Alberta. This is her first foray into storytelling.

Printed in Great Britain
by Amazon